How to Use
WINDOWS 95

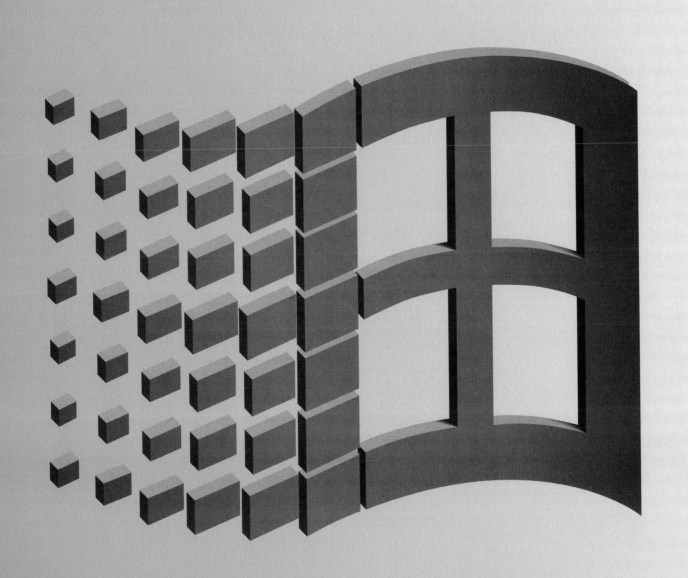

How to Use
WINDOWS 95

Douglas Hergert

Ziff-Davis Press
Emeryville, California

Editor	Stephanie Raney
Technical Reviewer	Mark Hall
Project Coordinators	Barbara Dahl and Cort Day
Cover Illustration and Design	Regan Honda
Book Design	Dennis Gallagher/Visual Strategies, San Francisco
Screen Graphics Editor	P. Diamond
Technical Illustration	Mina Reimer, Sarah Ishida, and Cherie Plumlee
Word Processing	Howard Blechman
Page Layout	Meredith Downs, Steph Bradshaw, and Joe Schneider
Cover Copy	Valerie Haynes Perry
Indexer	Carol Burbo

Ziff-Davis Press books are produced on a Macintosh computer system with the following applications: FrameMaker®, Microsoft® Word, QuarkXPress®, Adobe Illustrator®, Adobe Photoshop®, Adobe Streamline™, MacLink®Plus, Aldus® FreeHand™, Collage Plus™.

For information about U.S. rights and permissions, contact Chantal Tucker at Ziff-Davis Publishing, fax 212-503-5420.

If you have comments or questions or would like to receive a free catalog, call or write:
Ziff-Davis Press
5903 Christie Avenue
Emeryville, CA 94608
800-688-0448

ISBN 1-56276-268-0

Manufactured in the United States of America
10 9 8 7 6 5 4 3 2 1

To Elaine

TABLE OF CONTENTS

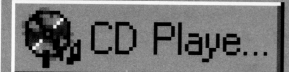 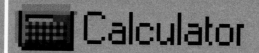 

ACKNOWLEDGMENTS

 For their expert guidance and support, I want to thank Cynthia Hudson and her team at Ziff-Davis Press: Barbara Dahl, Stephanie Raney, Lysa Lewallen, Carol Burbo, and Howard Blechman.

INTRODUCTION

 In all kinds of work places—offices, homes, schools, labs, and even spots as unlikely as lakeside resorts, airports, and coffee shops—Microsoft Windows has redefined the way people use their personal computers and laptops. Thanks to Windows, ordinary computer users are learning to work more efficiently and reliably than ever before. Even people who can't quite remember what GUI means (*graphical user interface*) are quickly coming to recognize the familiar visual tools of the Windows desktop. These tools are the basis for a more human and genial approach to personal computing—an approach that people everywhere have taken up with enthusiasm.

How to Use Windows 95 is an illustrated tutorial, introducing the latest version of Windows. If you're a newcomer to the system, this book will help you explore the software resources that Windows provides. In the first several chapters you'll master the basics—the Start button, the Taskbar, the desktop, and a variety of tools designed to help you adjust the Windows environment to *your* work patterns. Then you'll learn how to use Windows programs to accomplish specific tasks on your computer—produce documents, keep records, design graphics, manage schedules, perform calculations, play games, send e-mail, and more. Along the way, you'll actually *see* what Windows does and how it works. And because this book uses a *hands-on* approach, you'll learn by performing each step and task on your own computer.

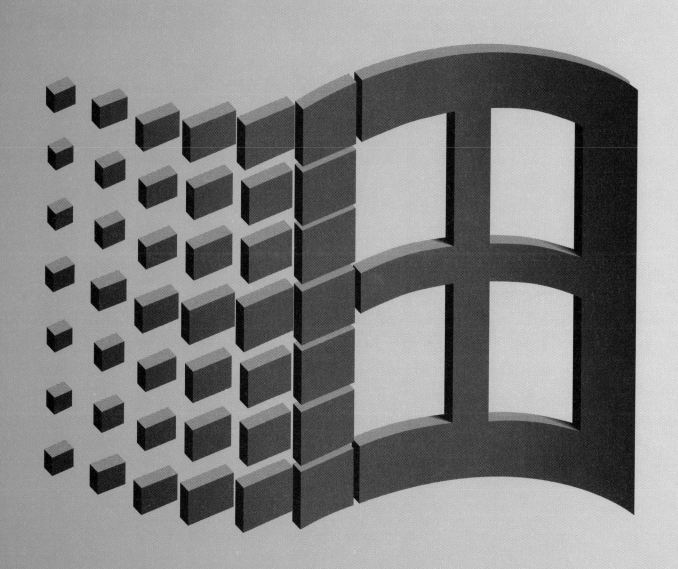

CHAPTER 1

Getting Started with Windows

There are many reasons for running Windows on a personal computer. Some people do so simply because their favorite application—a word processing program, a spreadsheet, or even a game—won't work without it. Other people run Windows to take advantage of a particular feature the software itself supplies—such as the Explorer or the Paint program that comes with the Windows package. Still others like Windows because it allows them to coordinate all their computer work in a single software environment—an environment that supplies a common set of simple mouse and keyboard operations as well as convenient ways to exchange information among programs.

You'll start out with your own particular reasons and you may find yourself amplifying those reasons over time. But no matter what you plan to use Windows for, there are certain basic features and skills that you'll want to master when you first begin. You'll need to know how to make your way around the "desktop" that appears on your screen; how to use the mouse and the keyboard; and how to select and run the programs that Windows puts at your fingertips. In this first chapter you'll begin developing these important skills.

How to Start Your Work

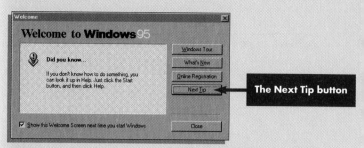

The Next Tip button

A few moments after you turn on your computer, Windows 95 takes control. Your screen becomes a visual "desktop," with a variety of pictorial elements (icons) available to represent your current work. When you eventually start running programs, your work will appear in individual windows. A window is a framed rectangle that encloses your activities in a particular program. As on an actual desktop, you can place many tasks on the Windows screen at once, and you can arrange your work in many convenient ways. The center of operations in Windows 95 is the Taskbar, which initially appears at the bottom of the screen. The Taskbar's Start button is key to many of the tools that Windows has to offer.

▶ **1** Turn on your computer and wait a few moments for Windows to get started. A Welcome window appears on the screen, with a brief tip displayed under the title "Did you know...." Before you close -Move the mouse pointer (a white arrow on the screen) over the button labeled Next Tip, and click the left mouse button. Each time you do so, Windows supplies a new tip. (**Note:** If the Welcome window doesn't appear on the desktop at the beginning of your session with Windows, this feature has been deactivated on your computer. See the Tip Sheet on these pages to learn how to reactivate it.) Click the Close button to close the Welcome window.

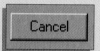

5 For now, click the Cancel button to close the Help window. For more information about the Help window, see "How to Get Help" in Chapter 2 of this book.

4 As a first experiment with the Start menu, click Help. In response, Windows closes the Start menu and opens a Help window. Click the Contents tab near the top of the window if it's not already selected. You'll see several categories of Help topics. You can now select any category and then click the Open button (at the bottom of the Help window) to view a list of topics or additional help categories.

▶ As you can already see, the mouse is an essential tool for making selections and starting programs in Windows 95. To learn more about basic mouse operations, turn the page.

▶ If the Welcome window doesn't appear on the desktop when Windows starts, you can view it by following these steps: Click the Start button and choose the Run command. Enter welcome in the box labeled Open, and then click the OK button. The Welcome window appears over your current work on the desktop. To make sure this window will appear at the beginning of each Windows session, click the small box at the lower-left corner of the window (labeled "Show this Welcome Screen next time you start Windows"). A check appears in the box. Click the Close button to close the Welcome window and resume your other work on the desktop.

2 Move the mouse pointer to the Start button at the lower-left corner of the desktop and hold it there for a moment. A small box appears with the message "Click here to begin." Windows often supplies brief explanations like this one when you simply hold the mouse pointer over a button you're thinking of clicking.

The Start menu

The Start button

The Taskbar

3 With the mouse pointer still positioned over the Start button, click the left button on your mouse to view the Start menu. You can now move the mouse pointer up and down the menu to highlight individual items in the menu list. The Start menu gives you access to programs, documents, and tools for changing the Windows settings. It also provides an entry point into the extensive built-in Help facility that Windows provides.

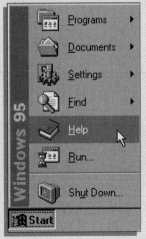

How to Use the Mouse

The mouse is indispensable in Windows. Using the mouse that's attached to your computer, you can get things done quickly, efficiently, and intuitively. Initially, the mouse pointer appears as a white arrow pointing diagonally up and to the left, but it often changes shape as you move to different parts of the Windows desktop or as you begin working in particular application programs. To select an item on the desktop as the object of a mouse action, you begin by positioning the mouse pointer over the item. You'll quickly learn to perform several basic mouse actions such as moving, pointing, clicking, double-clicking, and dragging. You'll also learn the different uses of the left and right mouse buttons in a variety of contexts.

TIP SHEET

▶ **The Taskbar (at the bottom of the desktop) displays buttons for all open windows, and gives you a simple way to select the window you want to work with next. See Chapter 2 for more information about using the Taskbar.**

▶ **When you maximize the size of an open window, the maximize button is replaced by the restore button, a small icon representing two overlapping windows. Click the restore button to return the window to its previous size.**

▶ **If you prefer to use the mouse with your left hand, Windows allows you to reverse the normal roles of the left and right mouse buttons. This switch can be a boon to left-handed people. For details, see "How to Change the Mouse Settings" in Chapter 4.**

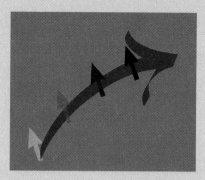

▶ **1** To *move* the mouse pointer to a new position on the Windows desktop, roll the mouse over a flat surface. The pointer moves in the same direction as the mouse.

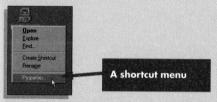
A shortcut menu

7 Using the *right* mouse button, click any object on the desktop (including the taskbar or the background area of the desktop itself) to view a *shortcut* menu. This menu contains useful commands that apply specifically to the object you've selected. In many shortcut menus, the Properties command allows you to change the appearance or behavior of a particular object. See Chapter 4 for more information.

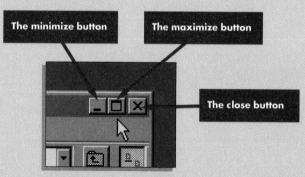
The minimize button   The maximize button
The close button

6 To change the appearance of a window, click one of the three buttons located at the upper-right corner of most open windows. Click the minimize button to clear a window temporarily from the desktop. (A button representing the window remains on the Taskbar; you can click this button to redisplay the window.) Click the maximize button to expand a window to its largest possible size on the desktop. Click the close button when you're finished working with the contents of the window.

2 To *point* to an item on the desktop, position the mouse pointer directly over the item. To *select* the item, click the left mouse button. For example, you can click the My Computer icon (at the upper-left corner of the desktop) to select it for a subsequent action; when you do so, Windows highlights the icon.

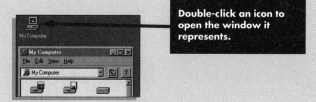

Double-click an icon to open the window it represents.

3 To *double-click* an item, position the mouse pointer directly over the object and then press the left mouse button twice in quick succession. Double-clicking is often a quick technique for opening a document or starting a program. For example, double-click the My Computer icon to open the My Computer window.

4 To *drag* an object, point to the item and hold down the left mouse button. Then move the mouse; as you do so, an image of the object moves on the Windows desktop. Finally, release the mouse button to settle the object in its new location. You can move the My Computer window by pointing to the blue title bar at the top of the window, and dragging the window to a new position on the desktop.

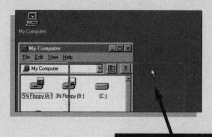

Drag a window by its title bar to move it to a new position on the desktop.

5 To *pull down* a menu in an open window, use the mouse to click the menu's name in the menu bar. You can then *choose* a command by clicking an entry in the menu. In response, Windows carries out the command you've chosen.

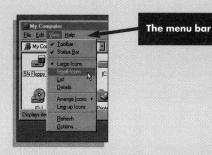

The menu bar

How to Start a Program

Once you know your way around the desktop, you're ready to begin experimenting with individual programs. The Start menu lists a variety of everyday application programs that come with the Windows package. Known informally as *accessories*, these programs include a simple word processor (WordPad), a drawing program (Paint), the Windows version of a hand-held calculator (Calculator), and several others. To start, or *run*, one of these programs you simply select it from the Start menu. A new window appears on the desktop for each program you run. The *active* window contains the program you're working on at any given moment. In the following exercise, you'll try running the Calculator, one of the most self-explanatory of the accessory programs.

TIP SHEET

▶ Windows allows you to run more than one program at once. Each running program is represented by a button on the Taskbar. In Chapter 2 you'll learn more about working with multiple programs on the desktop.

▶ You can use the keyboard to navigate the Start menu. To view the Start menu, press Ctrl+Esc. Press the up- or down-arrow key to select and highlight a menu entry. Press the right-arrow key to view another menu. When you've highlighted the program you want, press Enter to run it.

▶ The Calculator program has two built-in versions—the standard version, which you see illustrated on these pages, and the scientific version. Pull down the View menu in the Calculator window to switch between the two versions. Chapter 10 describes the Calculator program in more detail.

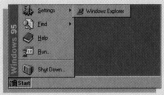

1 Click the Start button to view the Start menu. Then move the mouse pointer to the Programs entry at the top of the menu. When you do so, a menu of program names appears just to the right of the Start menu.Click the Start button to view the Start menu. Then move the mouse pointer to the Programs entry at the top of the menu. When you do so, a menu of program names appears just to the right of the Start menu.

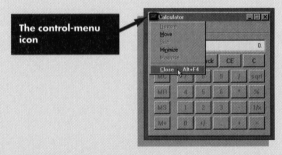

The control-menu icon

6 Close the application when you complete your work. A typical Windows program contains a File menu with an Exit command, but the Calculator program does not. To quit the Calculator you can simply click the Close button at the upper-right corner of the window. Alternatively, you can click the control-menu icon at the left side of the title bar and then choose the Close command.

2 Move the mouse pointer over to the Accessories entry at the top of the menu. The list of accessory programs appears to the right. Click the Calculator entry in this menu; in response, Windows runs the Calculator program.

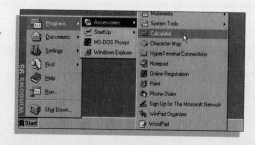

3 The application window for the program opens on the desktop. You can now begin working with the program. The Calculator contains buttons that look like those of an ordinary hand-held calculator. By clicking these buttons with the mouse, you can perform any kind of arithmetic calculation.

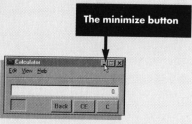

The minimize button

4 If you want to put your current work aside temporarily so you can focus on some other activity, click the minimize button at the upper-right corner of the application window. The program is reduced to a button on the Taskbar, and the desktop is cleared for any other activity you might want to start next.

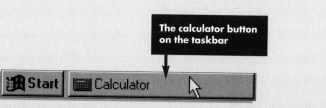

The calculator button on the taskbar

5 When you're ready to return to return to your work in a minimized application, click the program's button on the Taskbar. The application window reopens, displaying any work in progress just as you left it. For example, if you were in the middle of computing a result in the Calculator, you could now continue exactly where you left off.

How to Use the My Computer Icon

The My Computer icon, at the upper-left corner of your desktop, is designed to give you easy access to files stored on your hard disk or any floppy disk. Files on a disk can include documents you've created, or programs you want to run. In the terminology of Windows 95, files are organized in *folders* (previously known as *directories*). With a few clicks of your mouse, you quickly can open any folder on a selected disk and examine the files that the folder contains. Furthermore, you can *open* a file and begin running the corresponding program by double-clicking an icon within a folder.

▶ 1 Double-click the My Computer icon on the desktop. The resulting My Computer window contains icons representing your hard disk, floppy disk drives, and CD-ROM drive if one is installed on your computer. (It also displays some special Windows 95 folders that you'll learn about later.)

TIP SHEET

▶ You can change the way files are displayed in the My Computer window. To do so, pull down the View menu and choose one of the options in the second panel of the menu list. By default, files are depicted as large icons, but you can switch to small icons, a list, or a detailed table of file information.

▶ Windows 95 provides two other important programs you can use to explore the files on a disk: The Find program and the Windows Explorer. You can learn about both of these programs by turning to Chapter 5 of this book.

▶ You can use the My Computer window to create *shortcut* icons directly on the desktop for the programs and documents you use most often. Once you've created a shortcut, you can simply double-click it to start a program or open a document. See "How to Create a Shortcut" in Chapter 3 for details.

5 To close the My Computer window (or any related windows that have been opened as you examined the contents of your disk), pull down the window's File menu and choose Close, or simply click the close button located at the upper-right corner of a given window. The My Computer icon remains on your desktop.

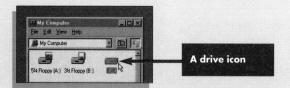

A drive icon

2 Inside the My Computer window, double-click the icon for the drive you want to investigate. In response, Windows displays a collection of icons representing the folders and files stored on the selected disk.

3 To view the files stored within a selected folder, double-click the folder icon. A folder may contain files alone, or a combination of files and other folders.

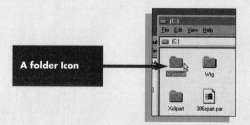

A folder Icon

4 To open a file, double-click its icon. If you select an icon representing a document file, Windows first runs the program in which the document was originally created and then opens the document inside the program. If you select the program file, Windows simply runs the program itself.

A document icon

How to Shut Down Your Computer

As long as your computer is on, Windows 95 remains in charge of operations. When you're ready to turn off your computer, you need to follow a few simple steps to end your Windows session in an orderly way. The Shut Down command is on the Start menu, just a mouse click away. When you choose this command, Windows conveniently checks all open documents to make sure you've saved any changes you've made. If any unsaved files are found, Windows gives you the opportunity to save them before you quit.

▶ **1** Click the Start button to view the Start menu. The Shut Down command is located at the bottom of the menu. Choose the Shut Down command.

TIP SHEET

▶ In previous versions of Windows, you returned to the DOS prompt whenever you ended a Windows session. This is not the case with Windows 95. In general, you quit Windows only when you're ready to turn off your computer.

▶ To run a DOS program, you can easily start a DOS session from Windows. To do so, click the Start button, choose Programs, and then choose the MS-DOS Prompt command. See Chapter 23 for more information about DOS.

▶ Any settings that you change during a given Windows session are retained for future sessions. See Chapter 4 for instructions on changing the appearance or behavior of the Windows environment.

5 Windows notifies you when it's safe to switch off your computer. (Alternatively, you can press Ctrl+Alt+Del to reboot your computer.)

2 The Shut Down Windows box appears on the desktop. Notice that Windows gives you three options: You can choose to shut down the computer, to start a new session with Windows 95, or to restart the computer in MS-DOS. The shut down option is selected by default; keep this selection if you're ready to turn off your computer.

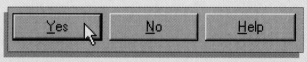

3 Click the Yes button if you're sure you want to end your current activities.

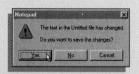

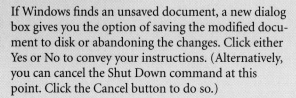

4 If Windows finds an unsaved document, a new dialog box gives you the option of saving the modified document to disk or abandoning the changes. Click either Yes or No to convey your instructions. (Alternatively, you can cancel the Shut Down command at this point. Click the Cancel button to do so.)

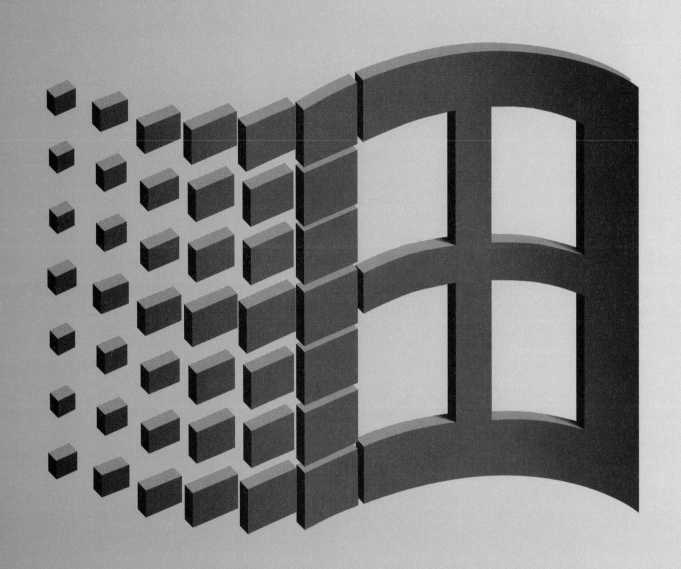

CHAPTER 2

Working on the Desktop

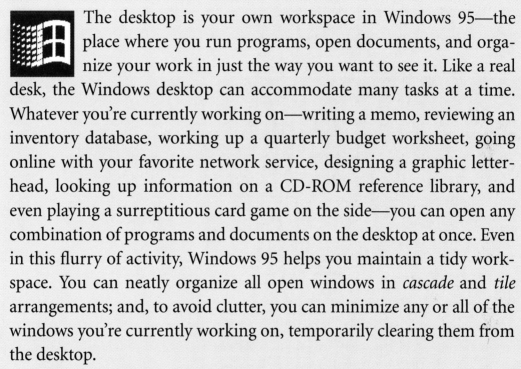 The desktop is your own workspace in Windows 95—the place where you run programs, open documents, and organize your work in just the way you want to see it. Like a real desk, the Windows desktop can accommodate many tasks at a time. Whatever you're currently working on—writing a memo, reviewing an inventory database, working up a quarterly budget worksheet, going online with your favorite network service, designing a graphic letterhead, looking up information on a CD-ROM reference library, and even playing a surreptitious card game on the side—you can open any combination of programs and documents on the desktop at once. Even in this flurry of activity, Windows 95 helps you maintain a tidy workspace. You can neatly organize all open windows in *cascade* and *tile* arrangements; and, to avoid clutter, you can minimize any or all of the windows you're currently working on, temporarily clearing them from the desktop.

Windows has an extensive built-in help facility to guide you in your work on the desktop. When you have a question about the steps of a procedure—or when you want to investigate a feature in greater depth—you can quickly look up the relevant help topic.

In this chapter you'll practice effective techniques for switching among the programs you run on the desktop. You'll also learn how to organize your work and how to get help when you need it.

How to Use the Taskbar

The Taskbar gives you a useful list of all the programs and documents that are open on the desktop. Whether you're working on one job or several at a time, the Taskbar displays a button for each program you're currently running. As you've seen, you can minimize windows to clear them temporarily from the desktop. When you're ready to work again in a program that's been minimized, you simply click its button on the Taskbar; the window instantly reappears on the desktop with your work intact. The Taskbar's shortcut menu—which you view by clicking the Taskbar itself with the right mouse button—gives you a variety of easy ways to organize your work.

TIP SHEET

▶ If you open many applications onto the desktop, you may begin to challenge the capacity of your computer's memory resources. To find out how much of your computer's memory is still available, pull down the Help menu in a Windows application and choose the About command. The resulting dialog box should show a message such as "System Resources: 54% Free."

▶ If you prefer, you can use the keyboard rather than the mouse to switch quickly from one application to another on the desktop. To read about this technique, turn the page.

▶ The first three commands in the Taskbar's shortcut menu (see step 3) provide quick techniques for arranging open windows on the desktop. For information about these commands, turn to "How to Arrange Windows on the Desktop" later in this chapter.

▶ Notice that the far right panel on the Taskbar is reserved for a display of the current time. If you hold the mouse pointer over this panel, a small popup box displays the current date.

▶ **1** To experiment with the Taskbar, begin by opening a selection of the Windows programs: Click the Start button and choose Programs from the Start menu. Then choose Accessories and click the name of a program you want to start. The program's window opens onto the desktop and a corresponding button appears on the Taskbar. Repeat this action for each program you want to open.

6 To close a minimized application without taking the time to restore its window on the desktop, click any button on the Taskbar with the *right* mouse button. Then choose Close from the resulting shortcut menu. If the window contains any unsaved work, Windows asks you if you want to save your document before quitting the program.

2 With several programs running at once, the task you want to work on may be temporarily hidden behind other windows. To *activate* a particular window, click the program's button on the Taskbar. The program you've selected comes to the front of the desktop, where you can resume your work in the active window.

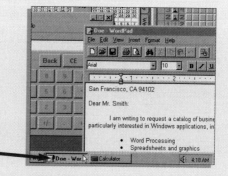

Click the button for the program you want to activate.

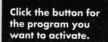

Click a blank area of the taskbar.

3 To clear all windows from the desktop at once, click a blank area on the Taskbar with the right mouse button. On the resulting quick menu, choose Minimize All Windows. All your current tasks are minimized, and appear only as buttons on the Taskbar.

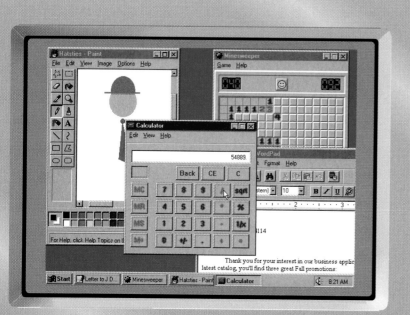

4 To restore one window to the desktop at a time, click any button on the Taskbar. The window reappears on the desktop with your work intact. To restore all tasks at once, click a blank area of the Taskbar to view the shortcut menu; then choose the Undo Minimize All command.

Click the up- or down-arrow button to see additional buttons on the Taskbar.

5 To continue this exercise, open some additional programs onto the desktop from the Accessories list. Each time you open a new program, Windows resizes the buttons on the Taskbar to make room for the new program buttons. If you finally open so many programs that there's not enough room on the Taskbar for another button, you'll see a small up-and-down arrow icon appear near the right side of the Taskbar. This icon indicates that the Taskbar's current contents are divided into two lists. To view the buttons for additional open windows, click the up or down arrow on this icon.

How to Switch between Applications

Even in a mouse-oriented environment like Windows, you may prefer to learn *keyboard* techniques for as many operations as possible. Lifting your fingers off the keyboard to click a button with the mouse sometimes seems inconvenient and inefficient. In particular, when you are running several programs at once, you may want to use the keyboard rather than the mouse to switch between applications on the desktop. Windows provides a simple two-key shortcut for activating a program of your choice.

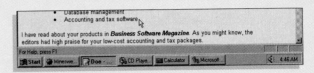

1 Start the applications that you plan to use during the current session with Windows. Optionally, maximize the active application to expand your work over the entire desktop.

TIP SHEET

▶ When you use the Alt+Tab shortcut to activate a window, the program you select is restored to its previous size and position on the desktop. If the application was maximized last time it appeared, it will be maximized again.

▶ If you are in the middle of using the Alt+Tab technique and you suddenly decide that you don't want to switch programs after all, press the Esc key once and then release the Alt key. The box disappears from the middle of the screen, and the current application remains active.

▶ You can use another keyboard technique to minimize, maximize, or restore the previous size of the current window. Press Alt+spacebar (that is, hold down the Alt key and strike the spacebar) to view the Control menu for the active window. Then press N to choose Minimize, X to choose Maximize, or R to choose the Restore command from this menu.

2 To switch to another application hold down the Alt key and then press the Tab key once. (Don't release the Alt key yet.)

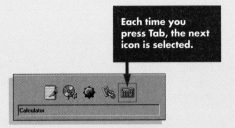

Each time you press Tab, the next icon is selected.

3 A box appears in the middle of the screen, displaying the icons of all the programs currently running on the desktop. While continuing to hold down the Alt key, press the Tab key one or more times to step through all the icons in the box. Each time you press Tab, a selection frame moves from one icon to the next. Beneath the row of icons, Windows displays the name of the application represented by the current icon.

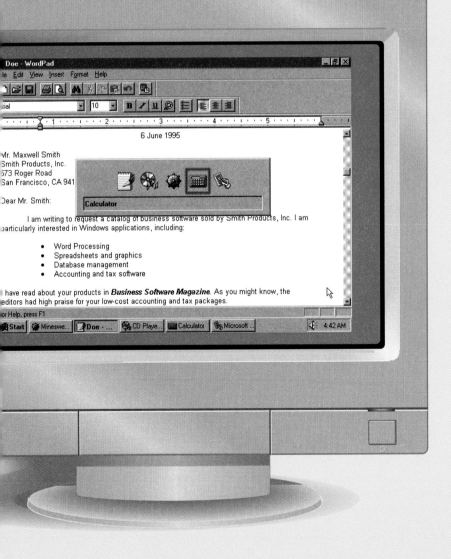

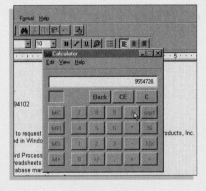

4 When you see the name of the program you want to activate, release the Alt key. The program you've selected becomes the active window on the desktop.

5 To open the Start menu and run a new program, you can use an additional keyboard technique: Hold down the Ctrl key and press Esc. The Start menu appears on top of your current work. Now use the arrow keys on your keyboard's number pad to select a program. Press Enter to start the program.

How to Arrange Windows on the Desktop

As you've seen already, clicking the Taskbar with the *right* mouse button results in a quick menu containing a variety of convenient commands. Among these commands are three options for rearranging open application windows on the desktop: Cascade, Tile Horizontally, and Tile Vertically. In the *cascade* arrangement, windows are "stacked" one on top of another. Because the windows overlap, only the front window is fully visible in this arrangement; others are identified by their title bars. In the *tile* arrangements, windows are automatically resized so they can appear side-by-side or one above another on the desktop. The more windows you include in the tiling, the smaller each window appears.

TIP SHEET

▶ **If you choose a cascade or tile command and then decide you want to return to the previous window arrangement, click the taskbar with the right mouse button and choose the Undo command from the quick menu.**

▶ **The cascade and tiling options are not the only ways to change the size and shape of an application window. You can also use your mouse to resize a window by dragging any border or corner of the window. When you position the mouse pointer over a side or corner of a resizable window, the pointer takes the shape of a two-headed arrow pointing vertically, horizontally, or diagonally. Hold down the left mouse button and drag toward the window's center to reduce the size, or away from the center to increase the size. (Note that this operation is not available for maximized windows.)**

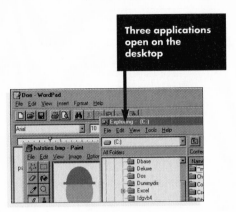

Three applications open on the desktop

1 Start the programs you want to work with. (Minimize any applications that you *don't* want to include in a cascade or tile arrangement.)

5 Finally, click the Taskbar with the right mouse button and choose Tile Vertically. You can see an example of this arrangement in the central graphic on these pages.

2 Move the mouse pointer onto a blank position on the Taskbar—that is, a position between two buttons, or between a button and the time panel at the right side of the Taskbar. Then click the right mouse button to view the shortcut menu for the Taskbar.

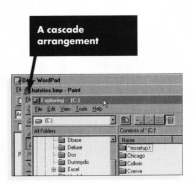

A cascade arrangement

3 In the shortcut menu, choose the Cascade option. In response, Windows arranges all the open applications windows in a cascade.

A vertical tile arrangement

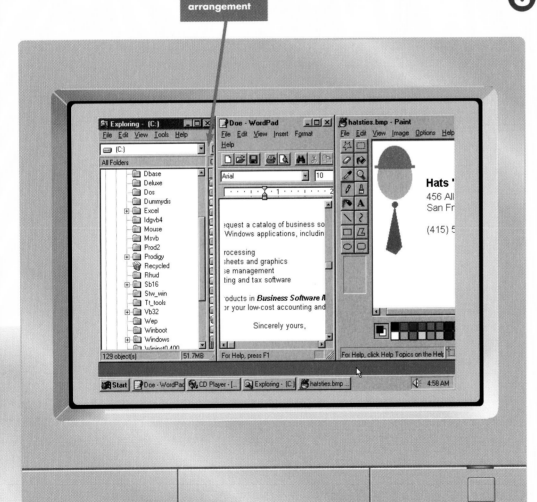

A horizontal tile arrangement

4 Click the Taskbar again with the right mouse button, and choose the Tile Horizontally command. Windows arranges the applications one above another on the desktop.

How to Get Help

Windows 95 provides a cross-referenced help system that you can turn to whenever you have questions about particular features or precedures on the desktop. The answers to your questions appear in specially designed Help windows. Information is organized by major topics and indexed intuitively by keywords. There are a number of convenient ways to open a Help window, depending on what you're doing when you decide you need help. A good place to start is the Help command in the Start menu. It provides several entries into the help system.

▶ **1** Click the Start button and choose Help. The Help Topics window appears on the desktop, as shown on the central graphic of these pages. Notice that there are three "tabs" displayed near the upper-left corner of the window; they are labeled Contents, Index, and Find. If the first of these is not already selected, click Contents.

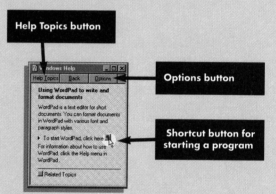

7 Some help topics contain special shortcut buttons that you can click to open a particular program onto the desktop. Click this button if you want to begin experimenting with the program that the topic discusses.

6 To look up a specific topic of your choice, click the Index tab in the Help Topics window. In the text box at the top of the Index box, enter the topic that you want to search for. Then select an index entry in the box below and click Display. In response, Windows opens a help window containing the information you've requested.

2 The Contents box contains a list of general topics, organized as "books." To open a book, click the general topic you want to read about and then click the Open button at the bottom of the Help window. A book may contain a combination of additional books, along with a selection of relevant help documents. Continue opening books until you find the document you want to read. Then select a topic and click Display to open it onto the desktop.

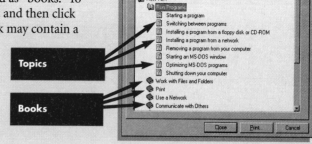

Topics

Books

Tabs

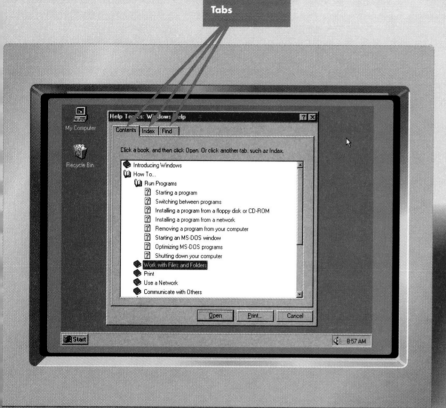

3 An individual help window typically provides you with the steps for performing a particular task. The window may also include tips and cross-references to related topics. In some topics you'll find special terms that are marked with dotted underlining. To see a definition, click an underlined term with the mouse. The definition appears instantly in a *popup* window. (To close the popup window, click anywhere on the desktop.)

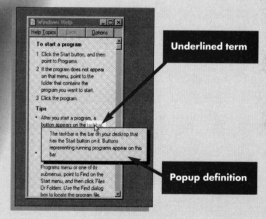

Underlined term

Popup definition

Related Topics button

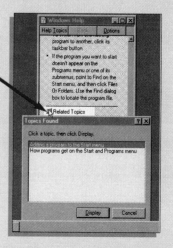

5 To return to the main help window, click the Help Topics button at the upper-left corner of a topic.

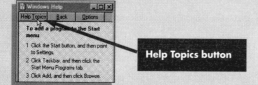

Help Topics button

4 At the bottom of most help topics, you'll find a Related Topics button. Click this button, and Windows provides a list of other topics you can go to directly. Select a topic in this list and click Display to read more information.

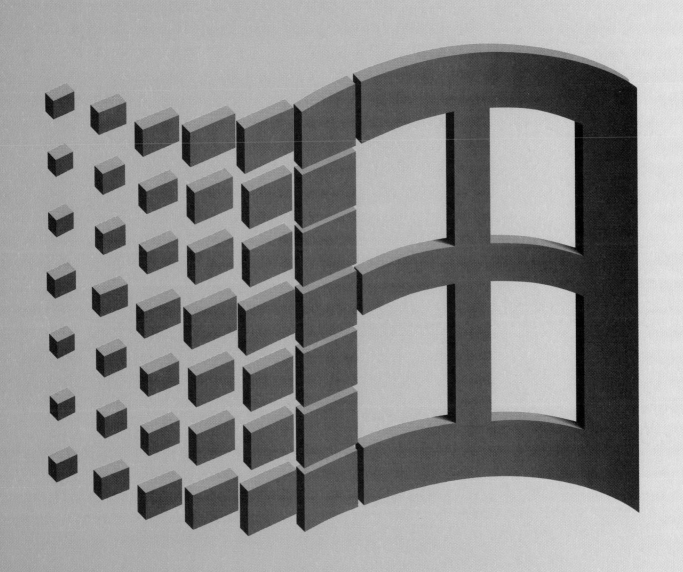

CHAPTER 3

Working with Programs

 From word processing to database management, from spreadsheets to Solitaire, applications are Windows' true *raison d'être*. Your own library of favorite applications may include programs that come with Windows, along with any variety of software packages that you buy separately to install and run on the desktop. The real purpose of Windows is to guarantee a consistent environment for all the programs you use on your computer.

Consistent is the key word here. By providing familiar mouse actions, convenient keyboard techniques, simple file-handling procedures, and intuitive visual tools on the desktop, Windows ultimately shortens the learning curve for each new program you run. Because the basic elements of the Windows environment are uniform from one program to the next, your own expertise is always on the rise. Whether you use two programs or 20, you can count on predictable operations for every task you perform.

In this chapter you'll examine a few of the important software elements that apply to all Windows programs including dialog boxes, document management procedures, and a variety of desktop tools related to programs and their documents. Starting with these features, you'll learn to work efficiently with programs in Windows 95.

How to Use Dialog Boxes

A dialog box is a framed group of options from which you make selections. This type of window appears on the desktop whenever a program needs specific information from you—often when you choose a particular menu command. (If a command name is followed by an ellipsis in a menu list, you know that a dialog box will appear when you click the command.) Dialog boxes contain several types of options that you'll quickly learn to recognize. You can select an option by clicking it with the mouse or by pressing the Tab key repeatedly until the option you want is selected. On these two pages you'll examine several typical dialog boxes from WordPad, the word processing program that comes with Windows 95.

TIP SHEET

▶ You can use keyboard shortcuts rather than the mouse to select many options on a dialog box. To do so, hold down the Alt key and then press the underlined letter in the option's caption. For example, press Alt+T to change the status of the Toolbar check box shown in step 4.

▶ In a dialog box that contains several command buttons, the *default* button has a heavier black border than the others. The OK button is often the default. To select the default, you can simply press Enter. Conversely, you can usually select the Cancel button by pressing Esc.

▶ To get help with a particular object in a dialog box, click the option with the right mouse button and then choose the "What's This" option. A popup box appears with an explanation of the option. Or you can click the question-mark icon at the upper-right corner of the window, and then click the object that you want to learn about.

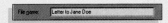

1 A *text box* elicits specific information from the keyboard, such as the name of a file or a numeric measurement. When you select a text box, a flashing vertical *insertion point* shows you where the text will appear when you start typing. When positioned over a text box, the mouse pointer takes the shape of an I-beam. To edit existing information in the box, click the I-beam at the location where you want to make an insertion or a change.

7 *Tabs* arranged along the top of a dialog box indicate that the window contains two or more "pages" of options. To view a particular page, click a tab with the mouse.

6 A *command button* represents an action or operation that a program can perform. To carry out the action, you simply click the button. Clicking the OK button is the usual way to confirm your selections in a dialog box. To close a dialog box without performing any action, click Cancel.

2 A *drop-down list* is a text box with an attached list of options. To view the options, click the down-arrow button that appears just to the right of the box. Then click any option in the resulting list. Windows copies your selection to the box located above the list.

3 A *list box* is simply a list of options from which you can choose. To make a selection, click any item in the list. Windows highlights your selection; if the list box is accompanied by a text box, Windows also copies your selection to the text box. (When a list box contains more options than can be displayed at once, a *vertical scroll bar* appears just to the right of the list. Click the up- or down-arrow on the scroll bar to view another part of the list.)

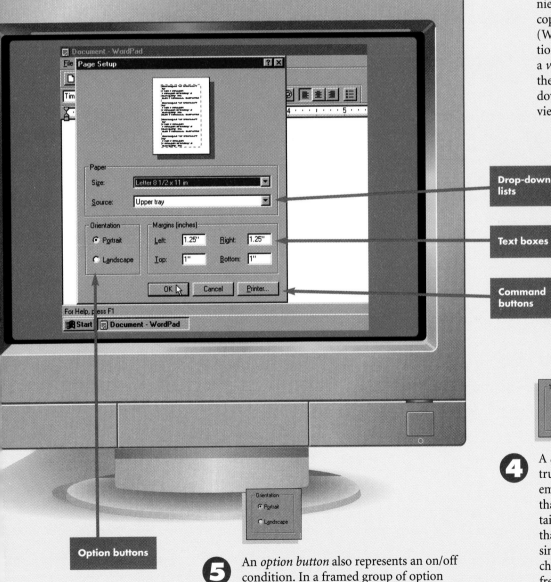

Drop-down lists

Text boxes

Command buttons

Option buttons

4 A *check box* represents a yes/no, true/false, or on/off condition. An empty check box indicates an option that is currently *off*; a box that contains a check indicates an option that is *on*. To change the status, you simply click the check box. Each check box is independent; you are free to select or clear any combination of these options.

5 An *option button* also represents an on/off condition. In a framed group of option buttons, only one can be *on* at a time; in other words, these options are mutually exclusive. To select an option, click it with the mouse; Windows automatically deselects any other options in the group.

How to Open a Document

A document is a file you create in a particular application. The type of information contained in a document depends on the nature of the application; for example, you can create a word processed document in Wordpad, a graphic file in Paint, or a worksheet in a spreadsheet program like Microsoft Excel. Windows 95 gives you a variety of convenient ways to open and manage documents. Most Windows programs have an Open command that you use to open a file from disk and display its contents in the work area of the application. The Documents list in the Windows 95 Start menu gives you a quick way of opening documents that you've worked on recently. In addition, the My Computer window allows you to open a document by double-clicking an icon.

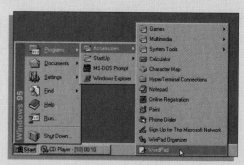

1 To open a document, you often begin by running the application in which the document was originally created. Click the Start button, choose Accessories, and then click the name of the application.

TIP SHEET

▶ You can place *shortcut* icons for frequently used documents directly onto the desktop. Then when you need to open a document, you simply double-click the corresponding icon. Turn the page to explore this technique.

▶ Windows 95 automatically adds a new name to the Start menu's Documents list whenever you open a document onto the desktop. You may occasionally want to remove the names from the Documents list. To do so, click the taskbar with the right mouse button and choose Properties from the resulting shortcut menu. Click the Start Menu Programs tab and then click the Clear button in the Documents Menu box. This action simply clears the Documents list; it has no effect on the actual document files you've stored on disk.

6 Alternatively, you can use the My Computer window to locate and open a document. When you double-click a document icon, Windows starts the application and opens the document. (See "How to Use the My Computer Icon" in Chapter 1 for further details.)

2 When the application window appears on the desktop, pull down the File menu and choose the Open command.

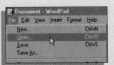

The My
Computer icon

Documents on
the desktop

3 In the Open dialog box you can begin by pulling down the Look in list and selecting the name of the drive on which the file is stored. If necessary, double-click the folder where you expect to find the document.

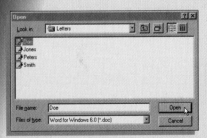

The Documents
list

4 When a list of documents appears, select the document you want to open. Then click the Open button (at the lower-right corner of the Open dialog box) to open the document and view its contents.

5 To view a list of the documents you've worked with recently on the Windows desktop, click the Start button and choose Documents. When you choose the name of a document from the resulting list, Windows automatically starts the appropriate application and then opens the document you've selected.

How to Create a Shortcut

Are there a few Windows programs that you use every time you turn on your computer? Or a set of documents—budgets, schedules, fax forms, memo templates—that you open on a daily basis? If so, you can easily place *shortcut* icons for these applications directly on the Windows 95 desktop. A shortcut gives you instant access to a program, a document, a folder, a printer, a disk drive, or any other object you use regularly in Windows. Once you've created a shortcut, you simply double-click it with the mouse to open the application that it represents.

▶**1** Open the My Computer window by double-clicking its icon on the desktop.

TIP SHEET

▶ **You can also use the *left* mouse button to drag a program icon from the My Computer window to the desktop. When you do so, Windows creates a shortcut icon without first displaying the shortcut menu shown in step 4.**

▶ **If you create a shortcut icon for your printer, you can then print any document by dragging a document icon to the printer icon. See Chapter 9 for more information about printing documents.**

▶ **By default, Windows arranges icons in neat columns, starting from the left side of the desktop. If you prefer to move icons around in a free-form arrangement (as in the central graphic at the right), click a blank area of the desktop with the right mouse button and choose the Arrange Icons command from the resulting shortcut menu. Then click the Auto Arrange command to turn this option off. You can now drag icons to any position you want on the desktop.**

▶ **To remove a shortcut icon from the desktop, you can simply drag it to the Recycle Bin icon. Turn the page for more information.**

5 Now to run the program or open the document, simply double-click the shortcut icon. The application window appears on the desktop.

2 By opening the appropriate drive and folders, locate the program or document that you want to create a shortcut for. Click the name of the file to select it.

3 Hold down the *right* mouse button and drag a copy of the selected application onto a blank area of the desktop.

A collection of shortcut icons on the desktop

4 Release the mouse button. When you do so, a menu pops onto the screen. Choose the Create Shortcut(s) Here command from this menu. In response, Windows creates the shortcut icon for the program or document you've dragged onto the desktop.

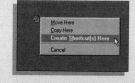

How to Use the Recycle Bin

You can delete files, folders, and shortcut icons from the desktop or from the My Computer window whenever you wish. But to safeguard against inadvertent deletions, Windows 95 maintains a special intermediate location called the Recycle Bin. Whenever you delete an object, it goes temporarily into this bin. If you later decide that you want to restore the object to the desktop, you can open the Recycle Bin window and choose the Restore command. Alternatively, you can empty one or more objects from the Recycle Bin when you're sure that you want to complete the deletion process.

TIP SHEET

▶ **Deleting a shortcut icon does *not* delete the application that the shortcut represents. The original program or document still exists on disk even after you delete the shortcut.**

▶ **Another way to delete an icon from the desktop is to select the icon and press the Delete key. Or, from the My Computer window, you can select an object and then choose the Delete command from the File menu. Whatever technique you use to initiate a deletion, Windows places the object in the Recycle Bin for safekeeping until you decide to delete it permanently.**

▶ **To change the way the Recycle Bin works, click the bin icon with the right mouse button and choose the Properties command from the resulting shortcut menu. The Recycle Bin Properties dialog box allows you to change the amount of disk space reserved for maintaining the Recycle Bin. In addition, you can activate an option called "Do not move files to the Recycle Bin" if you want to deactivate the Recycle Bin.**

▶ **1** To delete a shortcut icon from the desktop, use the mouse to drag the icon to the Recycle Bin icon. When the Recycle Bin is highlighted behind the icon you want to delete, release the mouse button. The shortcut icon disappears from the desktop.

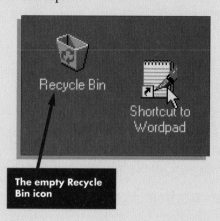

The empty Recycle Bin icon

6 Pull down the File menu. Choose the Delete command to carry out a permanent deletion, or choose the Restore command to return the object to the desktop.

2 To delete several shortcut icons at once from the desktop, begin by dragging the mouse in a rectangular area around the group of icons you want to delete. When you release the mouse button, all of the icons in the group are highlighted.

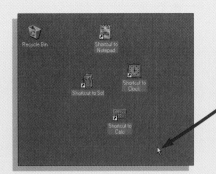

Select a group of icons by dragging the mouse pointer around them on the desktop.

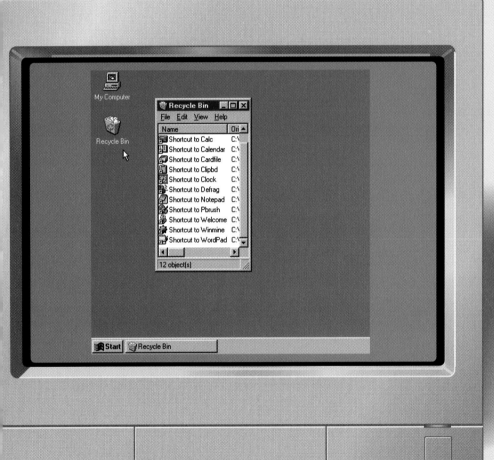

3 Now drag the whole group of selected icons to the Recycle Bin icon. Release the mouse button when the Recycle Bin icon is highlighted. The group of shortcut icons disappears from the desktop.

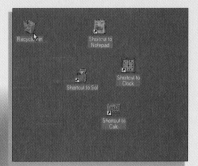

The Recycle Bin icon looks like this when it contains one or more files.

4 When the Recycle Bin contains one or more deleted objects, its icon is displayed as an overflowing trash can. Double-click this icon to open the Recycle Bin window.

5 To delete a file permanently from the Recycle Bin—or to Restore an object back to the desktop—begin by selecting its name in the Recycle Bin window.

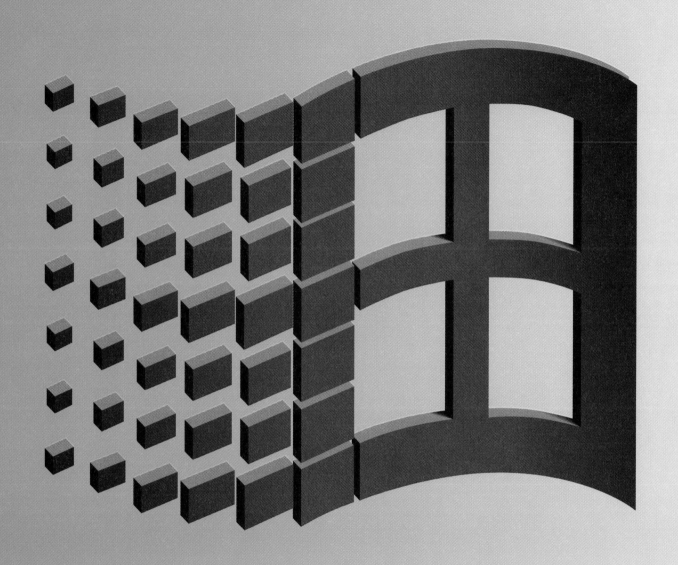

CHAPTER 4

Changing the Settings

 When you're ready to add a bit of flair and personality to the desktop—or, more importantly, to adjust operations to the way *you* like to work—you'll find that Windows provides many important options for customizing the interface. A few of these options are technical and best left to experts, but most are easy to use and fun to explore.

You begin by opening the Control Panel folder, which displays icons representing various changes you can make in the Windows environment. In this chapter you'll learn to select colors and patterns for the desktop; activate a screen saver; fine-tune the behavior of the mouse; and change the system date and time settings. You'll also learn to revise the contents and position of the Windows Taskbar and Start menu. Along the way, you'll gain a better appreciation of just how adaptable the desktop really is.

How to Select Screen Options

You may have several reasons for wanting to change the colors and patterns that appear on your desktop. Different visual effects can prove to be more soothing to the eye, or at least relieve the monotony of staring at the screen for hours on end. Or, your display hardware may simply produce better images with particular colors. Whatever your reasons, you can choose from predefined lists of patterns and color schemes that Windows supplies. In addition, you can install a *screen saver*, designed to prevent "burn-in" damage from long-term display of a single image on the screen.

TIP SHEET

▶ **Another way to open the Display Properties window is to click the desktop background with the secondary mouse button and choose Properties from the resulting menu.**

▶ **You can customize a color scheme by choosing your own preferences for specific elements of the desktop. Click the Appearance tab, select a desktop item, and then choose size, font, and color options for the item.**

▶ **Most of the screen savers can be fine-tuned for characteristics such as color, shape, and speed. Click the Settings button in the Screen Saver tab to make these changes.**

▶ **You can define a password to secure your computer from intruders while you're away from your work. Click the Passsword protected check box, and then click the Change button to define a password.**

▶ **1** Click the Start button and choose Settings. Then choose Control Panel from the Settings menu. The Control Panel folder opens onto the desktop.

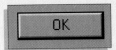

6 Click OK to confirm the selections you've made in the Display Properties window.

2 Double-click the Display icon in the Control Panel folder. The resulting Display Properties window contains four tabs representing various categories of screen options. The Background tab is selected initially.

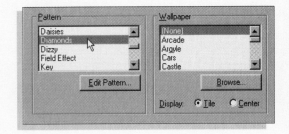

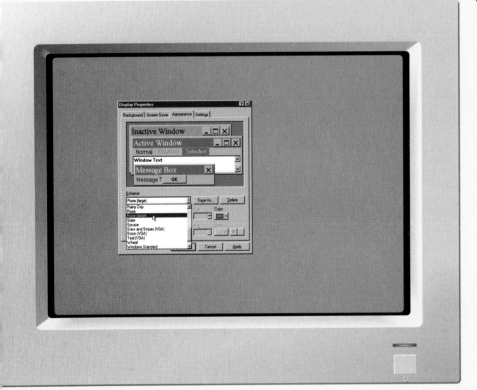

3 Scroll down the Pattern list and select the name of a predefined pattern. The sample screen shows what the desktop will look like with this pattern selection. Repeat this step until you've found a pattern you like, or select (None) to return to an unpatterned desktop. Alternatively, choose a graphic from the Wallpaper list, and click the Tile option to fill the desktop background with the selected image.

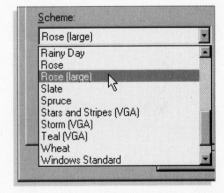

4 Click the Appearance tab at the top of the Display Properties window. Then click the down-arrow button at the right side of the Scheme box to view the list of predefined color combinations that Windows supplies. Select the name of a color scheme, and examine the results in the top half of the Display Properties window. Repeat this step to experiment with other schemes, or select Windows Standard to return to the original colors.

5 Click the Screen Saver tab and select an option from the the Screen Saver list. The sample screen demonstrates the appearance of the screen saver you've selected. Examine other screen savers until you find one you like. Optionally, change the numeric value in the Wait box. (Windows will activate the screen saver after your computer has been idle for the specified number of minutes; to clear the screen saver and return to your work, you simply press a key or move the mouse pointer.)

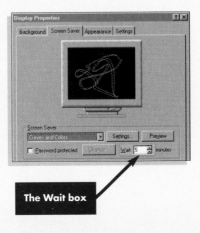

The Wait box

How to Change the Mouse Settings

Windows allows you to change several mouse characteristics, including the clicking rate required for a successful double-click; the *tracking speed* at which the mouse pointer moves across the screen in relation to the movement of the mouse itself; and the positions of the primary and secondary buttons on your mouse. By default, the primary mouse button is the one on the left, and the secondary button is on the right, but you can reverse these roles whenever you want. If you are left-handed, this may be one of the most important options available through the Control Panel.

TIP SHEET

► **When you select the Right-handed or Left-handed option and click the Apply button, the change in the roles of the two buttons takes place immediately. Any subsequent mouse operations—even within the Mouse Properties window—must be performed with the appropriate mouse button.**

► **As shown in step 6, the Motion tab offers an additional option, known as *pointer trails*. Activate this option by clicking the Show pointer trails option. Any subsequent movement of the mouse produces a trail of pointers. On some monitors this effect may help you keep track of the mouse's position on the desktop.**

► **The General tab allows you to reconfigure the type of mouse attached to your computer.**

1 Click the Start button and choose Settings. Then choose Control Panel from the Settings menu. The Control Panel folder opens onto the desktop.

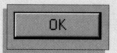

7 Click OK to confirm the changes you've made in the Properties for Mouse window.

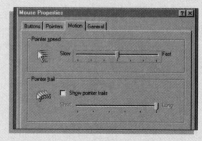

6 To increase or decrease the tracking speed, click the Motion tab at the top of the Mouse Properties window. Drag the slider toward Slow or Fast in the Pointer Speed section and then click the Apply button. To test the effect, move the mouse and notice the corresponding movement of the mouse pointer on the desktop.

2 Double-click the Mouse icon in the Control Panel folder. The resulting Mouse Properties window contains four tabs representing various categories of mouse options. The Buttons tab is selected initially.

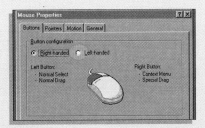

3 To reverse the roles of the mouse buttons, select between the Right-handed and Left-handed options. The mouse illustration shows you the current configurations for the primary button (used for "normal select" and "normal drag") and the secondary button (used for "context menu" and "special drag").

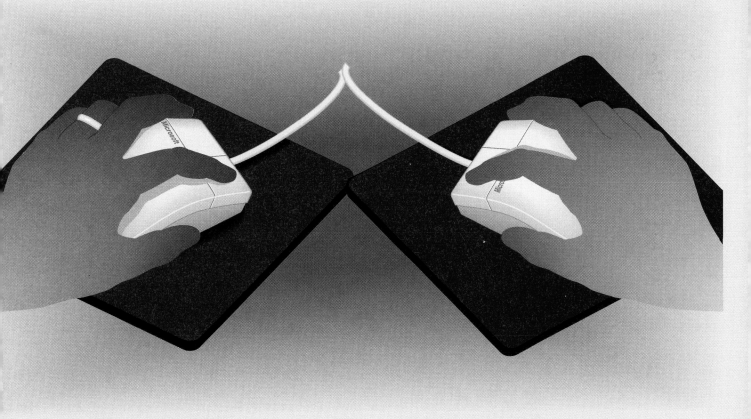

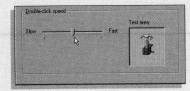

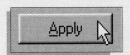

5 To increase or decrease the double-click speed, drag the slider toward Slow or Fast in the Double-click Speed section. To test the effect of this change, double-click inside the Test area. When the double-click action is successful, Jack pops out of the box.

4 To activate the new configuration immediately—without closing the Mouse Properties window—click the Apply button at the lower-right corner of the window. Use the primary mouse button for any additional selections you make in this dialog box.

How to Change the Date and Time

Your computer's internal clock and calendar supply the current time and date for many important operations. Individual applications use these settings for their own purposes. In addition, every file you save to disk is automatically "stamped" with the current date and time. You may need to adjust the time and date occasionally to keep them accurate. The Control Panel's Date/Time icon supplies the controls you can use to change these settings quickly and efficiently.

▶ **1** Click the Start button and choose Settings. Then choose Control Panel from the Settings menu. The Control Panel folder opens onto the desktop.

5 Click OK to confirm any changes you've made.

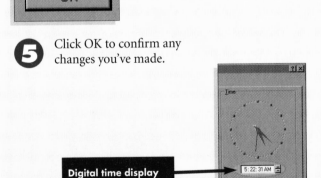

Digital time display

4 Check the current time to see if it is accurate. If you need to change any element of the time—the hour, the minute, or the second—double-click the appropriate digital value to select it. Then enter a new value from the keyboard, or click the up- or down-arrow button to increase or decrease the current value.

TIP SHEET

▶ **Another way to open the Properties for Date/Time window is to double-click the time display at the right side of the Taskbar.**

▶ **In the Time Zone tab of the Date/Time Properties window, you can select your time zone and automatically instruct Windows to adjust those settings for daylight savings time.**

▶ **The date and time formats are determined by options you can choose in the Regional Settings Properties window. (Double-click the Regional Settings icon in the Control Panel folder.)**

▶ **To view the current date at any time hold the mouse pointer over the time display at the lower-right corner of the desktop. A small tip box pops up to show the date.**

2 Double-click the Date/Time icon in the Control Panel folder. In the resulting Date/Time Properties window the Date & Time tab is selected initially.

3 Check the current date setting to see if it is correct. If you need to change the month setting, click the down-arrow button at the right of the month box, and select a new month. To change the year, click the up- or down-arrow button next to the year box. To change the date, click any entry in the calendar display.

How to Change the Taskbar

The Taskbar and the Start button are at the center of operations in Windows 95. Together, these two visual tools provide access to documents, programs on disk, and the applications that are currently running on the desktop. Because the Taskbar is so important, Windows gives you the opportunity to customize its use and appearance in ways that will suit your own work habits. For example, you can add entries to the Start menu for your most frequently used software programs. You can also control when and where the Taskbar appears on the desktop.

▶ ❶ Click the Start button and choose Settings. Then choose Taskbar from the Settings menu. The Taskbar Properties window appears on the screen. This window contains two tabs, labeled Taskbar Options and Start Menu Programs.

TIP SHEET

▶ **Another way to open the Taskbar Properties window is to click the Taskbar itself with the secondary mouse button and choose Properties from the resulting menu.**

▶ **To remove entries from the Start menu, click the Remove button in the Start Menu Programs tab. In the Remove Shortcuts/Folders dialog box, select the item you want to remove and then click the Delete button. (Windows copies the deleted items to the Recycle Bin, from which you can later restore them if you wish. See Chapter 3 for details.)**

▶ **To clear the current documents list from the Documents menu, click the Clear button in the Start Menu Programs tab.**

▶ **If you want the Taskbar to be hidden behind current applications on the desktop, click the Taskbar Options tab, select the Auto hide option, and click the Apply button. Windows subsequently shows the Taskbar only when you move the mouse pointer to the bottom of the desktop (or to the desktop position where you've moved the Taskbar).**

❻ To move the Taskbar to a different position on the desktop, use your mouse to drag it to the top of the screen, or to the left or right side of the screen.

❺ In the next window ("Select a Title for the Program") enter the program name just as you want it to appear as the new menu entry. Then click the Finish button. You can now run the program by selecting it directly from the Start menu.

2 Click the Start Menu Programs tab to create new entries in the Start menu itself. Then click the Add button in the Customize Start Menu group. The Create Shortcut dialog box appears on the desktop.

3 In the Command line box, type the full path name for the program you want to add to the Start menu. (Alternatively, click the Browse button if you want to search for the program's path on your hard disk. When you've found the program, Windows enters its path into the Command line box.) Click the Next button to continue this procedure.

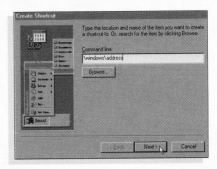

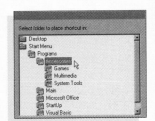

4 In the Select Program Group window, highlight the name of the folder where you want to display the new menu entry. For example, click Accessories if you want your program to be included in the Accessories list. Then click Next to continue.

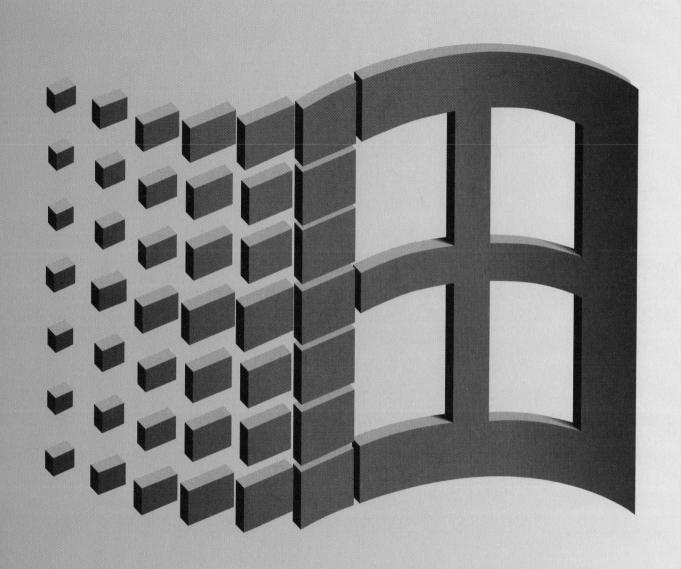

CHAPTER 5

Finding Files

If you've used DOS in the past to manage files on your computer, you've probably learned to perform a variety of everyday disk operations directly from the DOS prompt. For example, you may know DOS commands for listing the files in a directory (DIR), changing to a new directory (CHDIR), copying files from one place to another (COPY), renaming a file (RENAME), and deleting files (ERASE). Windows 95 provides *two* convenient programs for accomplishing similar tasks in a graphical environment—the Find utility and the Explorer. This chapter introduces you to both.

Before you begin, you need to be familiar with a few terms you'll encounter along the way. As you know, a *file* is the basic unit for storing information on a disk. A file may contain a *document* you've created within a particular application—for example, a word processed report, a spreadsheet, a database, or a drawing; or a file may store a program that you run on the Windows desktop. A *file name* is the unique identifier for a file. In previous versions of Windows, each file name was restricted to eight characters plus a three-character extension. Windows 95 lifts this restriction, allowing you to write free-form file names that are long enough to describe the contents and purpose of each file.

A *folder* is the new name for the structure previously known as a directory. Folders provide a way of organizing the space on a disk into practical divisions. A folder can contain any number of files, along with additional folders. The multilayered organization of folders on a disk is sometimes called the *folder hierarchy*.

How to Use the Find Program

Windows 95 supplies a simple but powerful tool that helps you find files, no matter where they are stored in your system. Using the Find program, you can search for files by name, size, category, date, or content. You can also search through all the folders on a given disk, or through specific folders of your choice. Once Find displays a list of files matching your search criteria, you can open any file—or start any application—simply by double-clicking an icon with the mouse.

TIP SHEET

▶ **If you want to search only in a selected folder, click the Browse button after step 2. In the Browse for Folder dialog box, navigate to the folder in which you want to search, and click OK.**

▶ **To search for files by date, click the Date Modified tab near the top of the Find window. You can search for files that have been modified within a specified number of days or months, or files that were changed between two specific dates that you supply. To search by other criteria, including type, size, and content, click the Advanced tab.**

▶ **To examine the contents of a document file without having to start the program in which the file was created, select the file in the Find window, pull down the File menu, and choose Quick View. The Quick View window can display a wide variety of documents, including word processing, spreadsheet, and graphic files. (If the Quick View command is not available in the Find program's File menu, the document you've selected cannot be viewed.)**

1 Click the Start button and choose Find. Then choose Files or Folders from the Find menu.

7 To start a new search, click the New Search button at the right side of the Find window. Then click OK on the Find Files dialog box.

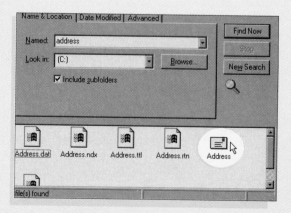

6 To open a file, double-click its icon. If the file is a document, Windows attempts to find the appropriate application in which to open the file. If you double-click the icon for an application, Windows starts the program.

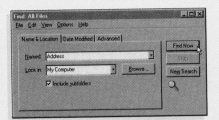

2 The Find window appears on the desktop. In the Named text box, enter the name (or part of the name) of the file or files you want to search for.

3 Pull down the Look in list, and select the drive location where you want to perform the search.

4 Click the Find Now button, located at the right side of the Find window. In response, Windows searches through all the folders on the selected drive for file names that contain the text you've entered into the Named box. During the search, a magnifying glass icon circles around the lower-right corner of the Find window.

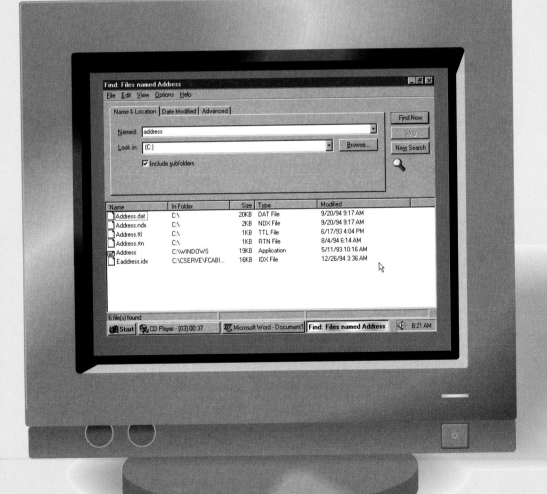

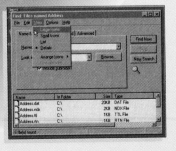

5 The Find window expands to display a list of the file names that match the text you've entered into the Named box. To view the files as icons rather than names, pull down the View menu and choose Large Icons.

How to Use the Explorer

When you start the Explorer, it displays two *panes* of information. On the left you see the hierarchy of folders on your current disk. You can quickly open any folder by clicking its icon in the list. On the right side of the Explorer window you see the contents of the current folder. Files in the contents list can be displayed as icons or as individual lines of text in a detailed table of information. They can be arranged by name, size, type, or date. The Explorer gives you simple techniques for copying, moving, opening, renaming, and deleting files in a selected folder.

TIP SHEET

▶ **Another way to copy a file is to begin by selecting the file in the contents list and choosing the Copy command from the Edit menu. Then select the folder or disk to which you want to copy the file and choose Paste from the Edit menu. Alternatively, hold down the Ctrl key as you drag a file from one folder to another; the mouse pointer is accompanied by a small boxed plus sign, indicating that you're performing a copy operation rather than a move.**

▶ **To delete a file, select the file in the contents list and choose Delete from the File menu (or press Delete on the keyboard). Then click Yes to confirm. To assign a new name to a file, select the file in the contents list and click its name once. Then type a new name from the keyboard.**

▶ **See Chapter 6 for information about creating new folders.**

▶ **1** Click the Start button and choose Programs. Then choose Windows Explorer from the Programs menu. The Explorer window opens onto the desktop. On the left you see the structured list of folders on your current disk, and on the right you see the contents of the current folder.

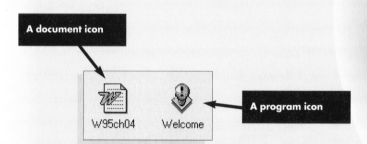

A document icon

A program icon

6 To open a document file, double-click its icon in the contents pane; if possible, Windows starts the appropriate application and opens the document. To run a program, double-click its icon in the contents pane.

5 To *copy* a file to another disk, use your mouse to drag the file from the contents list to the appropriate disk icon near the top of the folder list. (You may have to scroll to the top of the folder list before you begin this operation.) The original file remains in its source folder and a copy is created on the destination disk. To *move* a file to a new folder, drag the file from the contents list to a folder destination on the same disk. In this case, the original file disappears from its source folder. (See the Tip Sheet on this page for more information about copying files.)

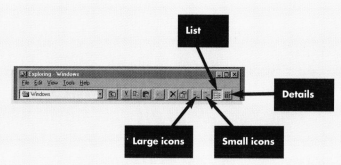

2 To open a folder and view its contents, click the folder in the list on the left. In response, the Explorer displays all the files contained in the folder you've selected. To expand the structure of a folder and view the list of folders it contains, double-click the folder's icon in the list on the left. You can change the relative widths of the two panes in the Explorer window by dragging the vertical split bar (displayed between the two panes) to the right or to the left.

3 If the Explorer's toolbar is not shown at the top of the window, pull down the View menu and choose Toolbar. Then click any of the last four buttons in the toolbar to change the way information is displayed in the contents pane. Click the Large Icons, Small Icons, or List button to view each file as an icon. Alternatively, click the Details button to view a table of information that includes the name, size, type, and date of each file in the current folder.

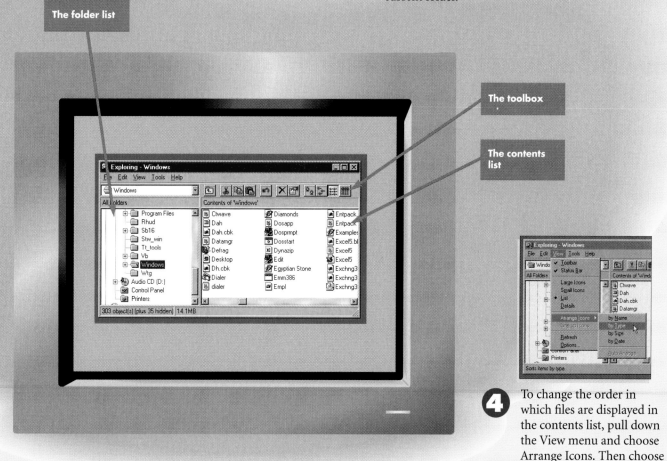

4 To change the order in which files are displayed in the contents list, pull down the View menu and choose Arrange Icons. Then choose one of the options in the resulting submenu to arrange the files by name, type, size, or date.

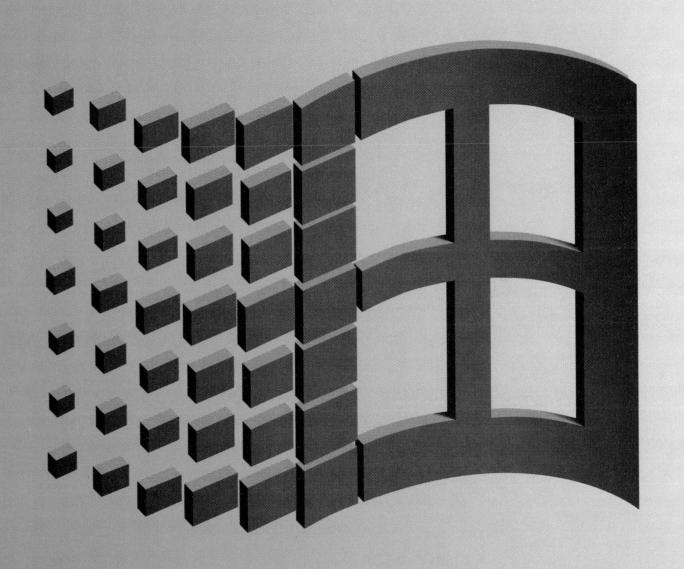

CHAPTER 6

Working with Folders

Folders give you a clear and simple way to arrange the files you create in Windows 95. In the My Computer window, the Find program, the Explorer, the Start menu—and on the desktop itself—folders help you systematically organize your work and efficiently locate files. You'll quickly become familiar with the small yellow icon that represents a folder.

As you know, folders were known as *directories* in previous versions of Windows and DOS. Given the large amount of storage space available on disks, folders provide an important structure for your files. You can create folders on any hard disk or floppy disk, or directly on the desktop. You can also create folders *inside* other folders. The many programs and documents stored on a hard disk are typically stored in a hierarchy of folders within folders.

Once you've created a folder for a specific purpose, you use applications such as WordPad or Paint to save new document files in the folder. Alternatively, you can copy or move existing files into a folder. In this chapter you'll learn to accomplish these and other folder-related operations. In addition, you'll discover a special location named the Startup folder, where you can designate programs that will be opened automatically at the beginning of each new session with Windows 95.

How to Create a Folder

You can use the My Computer window or the Windows Explorer to create a new folder on your hard disk or on a floppy disk. In either case, you begin by selecting the location for the new folder—at the top of a disk's folder hierarchy, or inside an existing folder. For convenient access to everyday files, you can even place folders directly on the desktop. Similarly, you can add new program folders to the Start Menu folder to expand the options presented in the Start menu itself.

1 To create a new folder in the My Computer window, begin by double-clicking the My Computer icon on the desktop. Then double-click the disk on which you want to create a new folder. Optionally, double-click one or more existing folders until you open the folder window where you want to create a new folder. (See "How to Use the My Computer Icon" in Chapter 1 to review these steps in greater detail if necessary.)

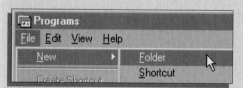

7 Double-click the Programs folder. The resulting window represents the contents of the Programs menu. Pull down the File menu, choose the New command, and then choose Folder to add a folder to the menu. Inside this new folder you can place any number of program shortcuts to provide access to a wider selection of programs from the Start menu.

6 The Start Menu folder contains a hierarchy of folders that define the contents of the Start menu itself. By inserting a new folder into this hierarchy, you can create an entry of your own in the Start menu. The Start Menu folder is located in the Windows folder on your hard disk. Use the My Computer window to find and open it.

TIP SHEET

▶ **Note that there are always two techniques available for adding a new folder to an open folder window: You can pull down the File menu and choose New, or you can click inside the window with the right mouse button and choose New and then Folder from the resulting shortcut menu. These two techniques are available in the My Computer window, the Explorer, or in any folder window on the desktop.**

▶ **To delete a folder, click the folder icon with the right mouse button and choose Delete from the resulting shortcut menu. On the Confirm Folder Delete dialog box, click Yes if you're sure you want to delete both the folder and its contents.**

▶ **To read about other techniques for customizing the Start menu, turn to "How to Change the Taskbar" in Chapter 4.**

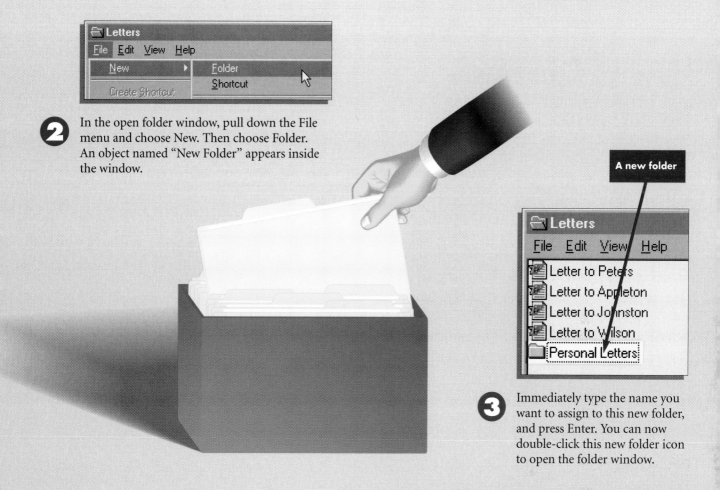

2 In the open folder window, pull down the File menu and choose New. Then choose Folder. An object named "New Folder" appears inside the window.

A new folder

3 Immediately type the name you want to assign to this new folder, and press Enter. You can now double-click this new folder icon to open the folder window.

4 Alternatively, you can use the Explorer to create a new folder. Click the Start button, choose Programs, and then choose Windows Explorer. In the left-hand panel of the Explorer window, click the disk or folder in which you want to create a new folder. Then move the mouse pointer inside the right-hand panel, and click the *right* (or secondary) mouse button to view the shortcut menu for this window. Choose New and then Folder from the menu. A new folder appears in the panel. Type the name you want to assign to the folder and press Enter.

5 To create a new folder on the desktop, click the right mouse button at any empty position on the desktop. Choose New and then Folder from the resulting shortcut menu. A folder appears on the desktop. Type the name you want to assign the folder, and press Enter.

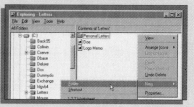

A folder on the desktop

How to Add Items to a Folder

The applications in which you create document files—such as WordPad, Excel, or Paint—all provide a Save As command in the File menu. When you choose this command to store your current work to disk, your first task is to decide where you want to save the file—that is, what folder to open for the save operation. For this purpose, the Save As dialog box gives you a clear way to select a folder from any disk. But you can also move (or copy) *existing* files to a new folder, as a way of reorganizing the work you've already stored on disk.

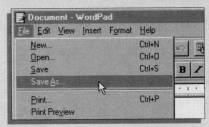

1 In any application designed for creating documents, pull down the File menu and choose Save As to store your current work on disk for the first time.

TIP SHEET

▸ **You can also conveniently use the Windows Explorer to move or copy files from one folder to another. See "How to Use the Explorer" in Chapter 5 for details.**

▸ **When files are displayed as icons in a folder window, you can select multiple files by dragging the mouse in a rectangular selection area around the target files.**

▸ **When you drag a file from one folder to another, the destination folder does not necessarily have to be open as a window. As illustrated in step 5, you can simply drag the target file (or files) onto the folder icon.**

Moving several files at once to a new folder

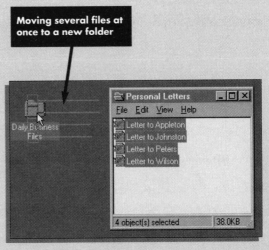

5 To select multiple files for a move operation, open the source folder and hold down the Ctrl key while you click each target file in turn. Then drag the files all at once to the destination folder. (To *copy* the files, hold down the Ctrl key while you drag.)

2 In the Save As dialog box, double-click the icon for the folder in which you want to save your work. Windows copies the name of the folder to the Save in box. To complete the save operation, enter a file name and click the Save button.

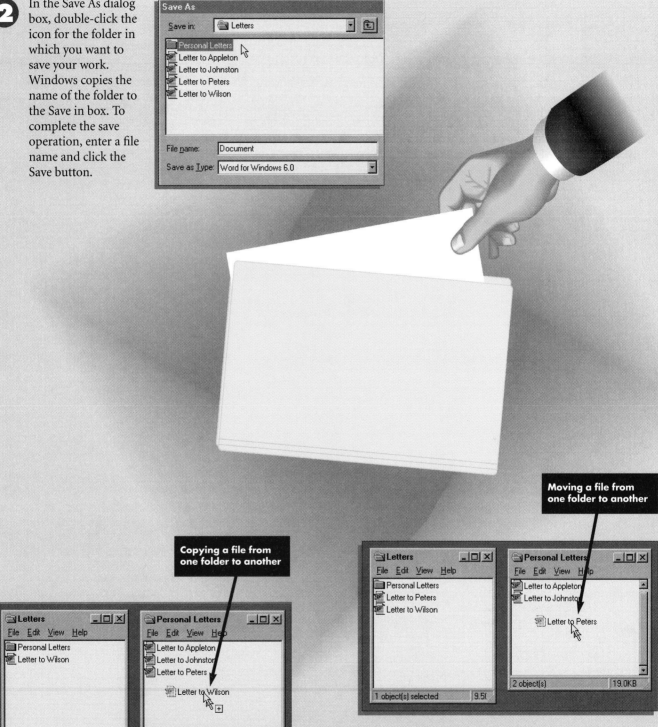

Copying a file from one folder to another

Moving a file from one folder to another

3 To move a file from one folder to another, use the My Computer tool to open windows for both the source folder and the destination folder, and then drag the target file from one folder to another.

4 To copy a file from one open folder window to another, hold down the Ctrl key while you drag the file from its source to its destination.

How to Designate Startup Applications

S tartup is a special folder that allows you to define *automatic applications*—programs that will be started at the beginning of every Windows session. You can place shortcut icons in the Startup folder for the applications you use every day. By doing so, you save yourself the trouble of having to start these applications yourself when you begin your work.

▶ **1** Use the My Computer window to open the Start Menu folder from the Windows folder.

5 Repeat steps 3 and 4 for any additional programs you want to place in the Startup folder. Then close the Startup window. Next time you start Windows, all the programs in your Startup folder will automatically open onto the desktop.

TIP SHEET

▶ **You can also drag icons from other folders into the Startup folder, as described in "How to Add Items to a Folder" (the previous page in this chapter). Windows creates shortcuts rather than copies of the target programs.**

▶ **If you decide you no longer want an application to start automatically, you can delete the program's icon from the Startup folder. To do this, open the folder, select the icon you want to delete, and press Del on the keyboard. Windows asks you to confirm the deletion; click the Yes button in the Delete box if you're sure you want to delete the icon.**

▶ **See "How to Change the Taskbar" in Chapter 4 for another approach to revising the Start Menu and the Startup folder.**

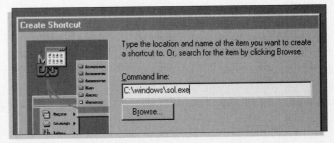

4 Enter the full path of the program you want to add to the Startup folder. Then click Next and enter a name for identifying the program. Click Finish to complete the operation.

2 Double-click the Programs folder. Then, inside the Programs folder, double-click the Startup folder. The Startup window appears on the desktop. If you haven't designated any startup programs yet, the folder is empty.

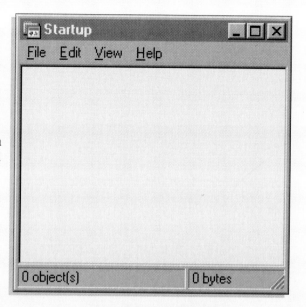

3 Move the mouse pointer into the Startup window, and click the right mouse button. From the resulting shortcut menu choose New and then Shortcut. The Create Shortcut dialog box appears.

These programs will start automatically at the beginning of each session with Windows.

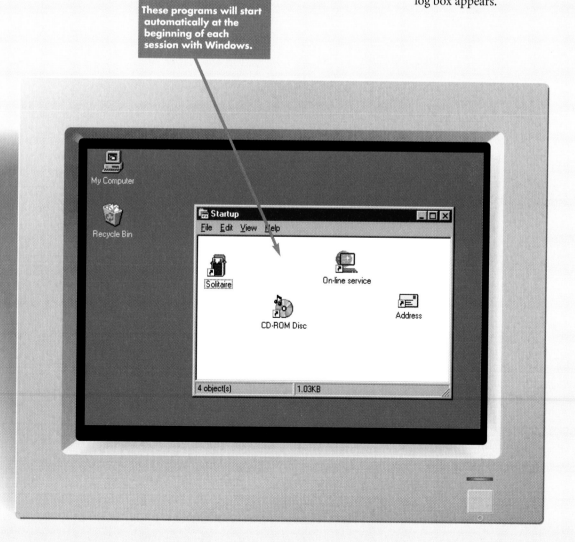

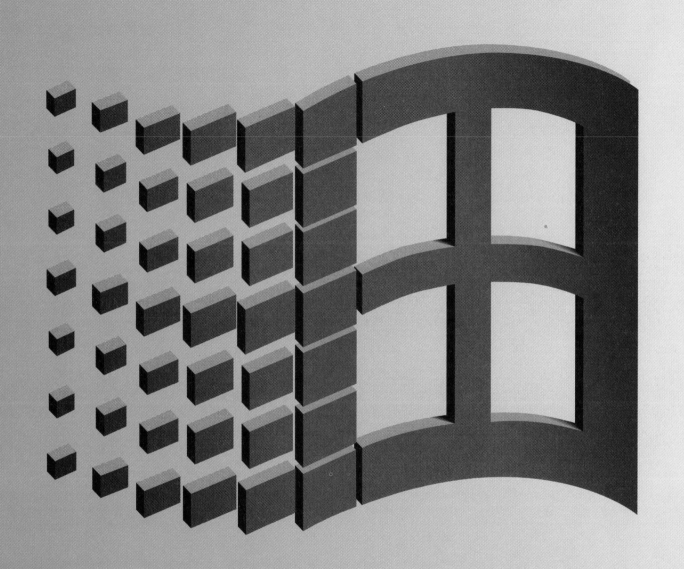

CHAPTER 7

Word Processing

Word processing has forever changed the lives of people who write. Whatever you put down on paper—letters, memos, reports, speeches, essays, stories, poems, plays, novels, recipes, grocery lists, homework assignments, term papers, dissertations, or your personal journal—word processing simplifies your work and inevitably improves the result. A good word processing program gives you tools to streamline every step along the way—from composing the initial draft, to revising and correcting the text, to producing attractive and readable copy on paper.

WordPad is the name of the word processing program that comes with Windows 95. It's simple enough to master in a short time, yet has the features you need for most day-to-day word processing tasks. This chapter introduces you to some of the most important WordPad procedures. You'll learn how to type and correct the text of a document, select typographical effects to make your text easier to read, and format paragraphs in your document. You'll also see how to save your work as a file on disk and print it onto paper.

As in other Windows applications, the feature known as the Clipboard allows you to copy or move information from one place to another within a WordPad document or from one document to another. You can use copy-and-paste and cut-and-paste procedures to transfer text or graphics. You'll learn about these procedures in Chapter 8. In addition, Chapter 14 introduces you to several other word processing techniques.

How to Get Started in WordPad

If you've never used a word processor before, you'll be pleasantly surprised at how easy it is to get started in WordPad. You simply start the application and begin typing, almost as you would on a typewriter. But there are several big differences between a typewriter and a word processor. Most importantly, the WordPad application makes it very easy for you to revise your work. You use the mouse or the keyboard to move to any part of your document; then you can insert new text or erase parts of the text that you've already typed.

1 Click the Start button and choose Programs. From the Programs menu, choose Accessories. Then choose WordPad from the Accessories menu.

TIP SHEET

▶ **To insert new text in an existing section of your document, use the mouse or keyboard to move the insertion point, and start typing. (Press Enter to create a new paragraph within the existing text.)**

▶ **To abandon the current document and start a new one, click New, the first button on the Toolbar. In the resulting New dialog box, select a document type and then click OK. (Word 6 Document is the standard document type.) Then click No when WordPad asks you if you want to save changes in the current document.**

▶ **Like all major Windows applications, WordPad has its own online help. To see the list of available topics, pull down the Help menu and choose Help Topics.**

▶ **To close WordPad, pull down the File menu and choose Exit.**

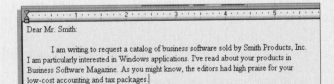

5 Press Enter to start a new paragraph. (Optionally, press Enter again to insert a blank line into your document.) Then press Tab to indent. Try typing a paragraph containing two or three lines of text. When you reach the end of a line, notice that WordPad automatically moves the insertion point to the beginning of the next line. In other words, you do *not* press the Enter key to start a new line within a paragraph; the *word-wrap* feature takes you to the next line automatically.

2 The WordPad application window appears on the desktop. At the top of the window, the title bar displays the generic name "Document" to identify your work in this window. (After you save your work to disk, the title bar will display the actual name you assign to the current document file.) Click the Maximize button at the right side of the title bar to expand the window over the entire available desktop space.

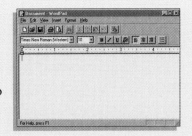

Toolbar

Format bar

Ruler

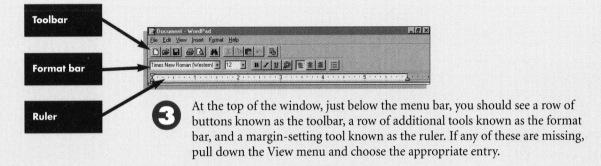

3 At the top of the window, just below the menu bar, you should see a row of buttons known as the toolbar, a row of additional tools known as the format bar, and a margin-setting tool known as the ruler. If any of these are missing, pull down the View menu and choose the appropriate entry.

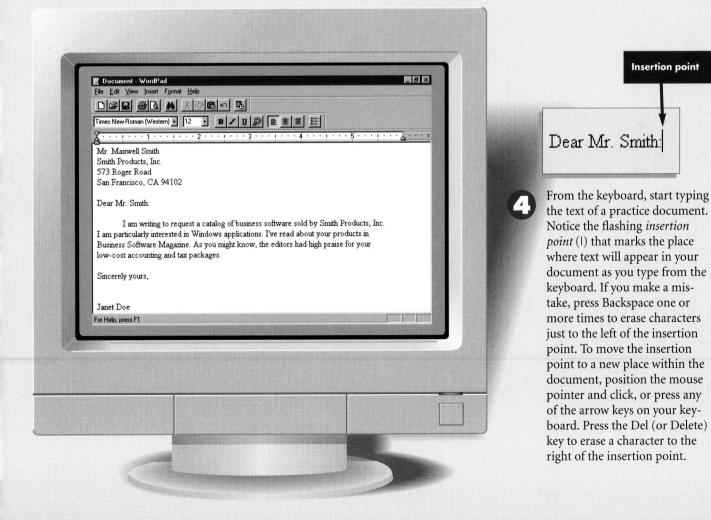

Insertion point

Dear Mr. Smith:

4 From the keyboard, start typing the text of a practice document. Notice the flashing *insertion point* (I) that marks the place where text will appear in your document as you type from the keyboard. If you make a mistake, press Backspace one or more times to erase characters just to the left of the insertion point. To move the insertion point to a new place within the document, position the mouse pointer and click, or press any of the arrow keys on your keyboard. Press the Del (or Delete) key to erase a character to the right of the insertion point.

How to Apply Styles, Fonts, and Colors

Special typographical effects—including styles, sizes, fonts, and colors—can enhance the appearance of documents you create in WordPad. To apply these effects, you select the target text and then choose specific options from the format bar near the top of the WordPad window. For example, you can apply boldface, italic, and underlining styles—individually or in combinations—to any selection of text. In addition, you can increase or decrease the type size and change the font, or typeface design, in an entire document or a selected portion of it. As a final touch, you can add color to make a document even more attractive and appealing.

TIP SHEET

▸ **If you prefer, you can use the keyboard to select text. Move the insertion point to the beginning or end of the text you want to select. Then hold down the Shift key and press the Right or Left Arrow key repeatedly to select text within a line, or the Up or Down Arrow key to select entire lines.**

▸ **Press Ctrl+A to select the entire contents of the current document.**

▸ **To identify a button displayed on the toolbar or the format bar, simply position the mouse pointer over the button itself. In response, WordPad displays a small "ToolTip" box that tells you what the button does.**

▸ **If you prefer, you can choose styles, fonts, sizes, and colors from a dialog box. Select the target text, pull down the Format menu, and choose the Font command. The resulting dialog box contains the formatting options available in WordPad.**

▶ **①** Hold down the left (or primary) mouse button and drag the mouse over the text where you want to apply a style, size, font, or color. To select a line or part of a line, drag the mouse horizontally. To select all or part of multiple lines, drag the mouse vertically. (See the Tip Sheet on this page for additional text-selection techniques.) Your selection is *highlighted*—that is, displayed as white text against a dark background.

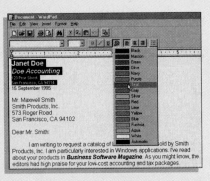

⑤ To change the color of the selected text, click the Color button on the format bar, and choose the color that you want to apply.

④ To change the font of the selected text, click the down-arrow button next to the Font box on the format bar, and choose the name of a new font from the resulting list. (*TrueType* fonts are marked with a double-T icon. These are normally the best choice for WordPad documents, because you can rely on them to look the same on paper as they do on the screen.)

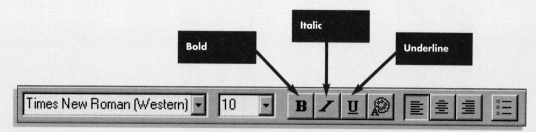

2 To apply one or more styles to the selected text, click the Bold, Italic, and/or Underline buttons on the format bar. For example, you can produce bold italic text by clicking the Bold and Italic buttons. (Note that Ctrl+B, Ctrl+I, and Ctrl+U are the keyboard shortcuts for applying boldface, italics, and underlining to a selection of text.)

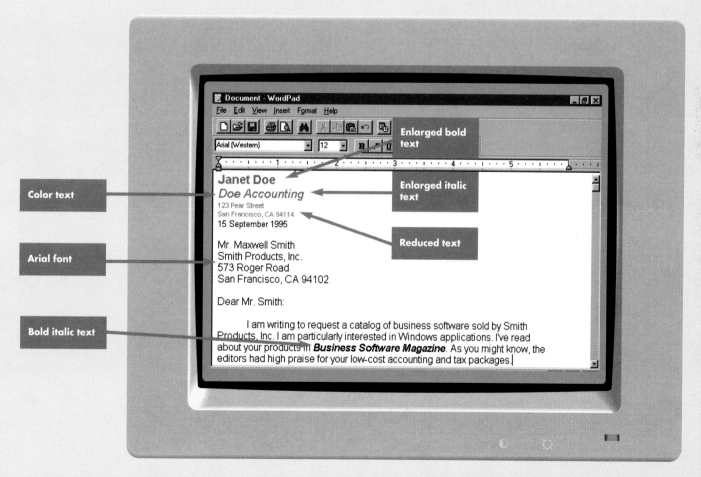

3 To change the size of the selected text, click the down-arrow button next to the Font Size box on the format bar, and choose a new point size from the resulting list.

How to Format Paragraphs

WordPad's format bar and ruler provide convenient tools for changing the alignment of text and for adjusting the paragraph-indent settings. By default, text is left-aligned, which means that each new line of text begins at the left margin. With the click of a button, you can center or right-align any single line of text or all the lines of a paragraph. Changing the left and right indent settings of a paragraph is as simple as sliding markers to new positions along the Ruler. Finally, you can add bulleted lists to a document by starting a new line and clicking the Bullet button on the format bar.

TIP SHEET

▶ At the left side of the Ruler, the first-line indent marker and the left indent marker are displayed as two small triangles, one on top of the other. These markers can move independently; use your mouse to drag them to new positions along the Ruler. To move both markers together, drag the small square marker displayed just below them (as illustrated in step 5).

▶ To change the indent settings for an entire document, pull down the Edit menu and choose the Select All command—or simply press Ctrl+A—to select all the text of the document. Then slide the markers to new positions along the Ruler.

▶ *Margins* define the blank areas along the top, bottom, left, and right sides of the printed page. (By contrast, the indent settings represent paragraph offsets within the current margins.) To change the margins of a document, pull down the File menu and choose the Page Setup command. Then enter new measurement settings in the Top, Bottom, Left, and Right boxes.

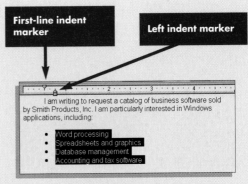

1 To change the alignment of one or more paragraphs, select the text and then click the Align Left, Center, or Align Right button on the format bar. (Notice that a "paragraph" may consist of a single line of text ending with a carriage return.)

5 To change the left-indent setting of a bulleted list, select all the lines of the list and then drag the square left-indent marker to a new position along the Ruler. (See the Tip Sheet on this page for more information about left-indent markers.)

2 To adjust the right-indent setting of one or more paragraphs, begin by selecting the text that you want to change. Then slide the right-indent marker to a new position along the Ruler.

Right indent marker

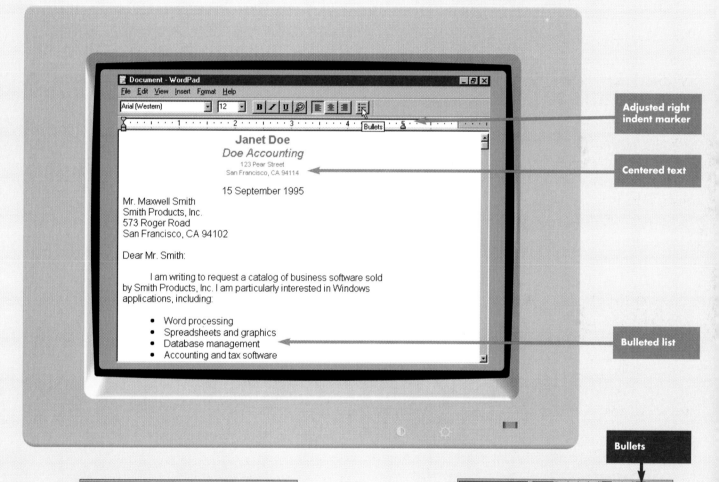

Adjusted right indent marker

Centered text

Bulleted list

Bullets

4 To continue a list, simply press Enter at the end of each bulleted line of text. WordPad automatically supplies a bullet for each new entry in the list. (To end the list, press Enter after the last line and then click the Bullets button on the format bar again; WordPad deletes the last bullet.)

3 To create a bullet, press Enter to start a new line and then click the Bullets button on the format bar. (WordPad automatically sets up a *hanging indent*, in which the first line of each bulleted paragraph starts further to the left than any subsequent lines.)

How to Save a WordPad File

The more time you spend composing a document, the more frequently you'll want to save your work to disk. The first time you save, Windows gives you the opportunity to supply a meaningful name for the file. After that, each save operation updates the file with the latest version of your document. Unlike previous operating environments for PCs, Windows 95 allows long, multiword file names. For example, you can name a file "Smith Catalog Request" rather than just SMITH.DOC.

▶ **1** Click the Save button on the toolbar. If this is the first time you've saved this document, WordPad displays the File Save As dialog box on the desktop, as shown in the central graphic on these pages.

6 As you continue to work on this document, click the Save button on the toolbar from time to time to update your work on disk. (Alternatively, pull down the File menu and choose Save, or press Ctrl+S from the keyboard.)

5 Click the Save button to complete the Save operation.

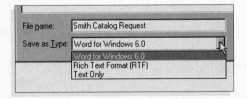

4 Notice the setting in the Save as type box. By default, WordPad saves your files in the format used by Microsoft Word for Windows 6.0. If you want to save the current file in a different format, click the down-arrow button at the right side of the box and select the name of one of the other available formats.

TIP SHEET

▶ **For more information about folders and files, turn back to Chapter 6.**

▶ **To reopen a WordPad file that you've saved in a previous session with the program, click Open, the second button displayed on the toolbar. The File Open dialog box displays a list of all the WordPad files in the current directory. Select the file you want to open and click the OK button.**

▶ **Alternatively, the File menu displays a short list of the most recent files you've worked with in WordPad. To reopen one of these documents, pull down the File menu and choose the name of the file you want to open.**

2 If you want to save your file on a disk other than the current one, pull down the Save in list by clicking the down-arrow button at the right side of the box, and make a selection. The box beneath the Save in list displays the names of all the folders on the disk you've selected. To open a particular folder for the current save operation, double-click a folder icon of your choice.

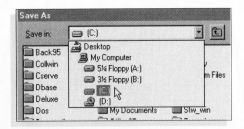

3 In the File name text box, type a name for your file.

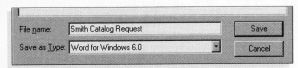

How to Print a WordPad Document

Your final goal in WordPad is to produce an attractive paper document that you can mail to a friend, distribute to your colleagues, fax to a client, or maybe even submit to a publisher. When you're ready to print a document, the first and most obvious step is to make sure your printer is on. After that, you can open the document and begin printing.

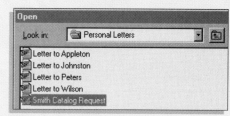

▶ **①** If the file you want to print isn't open yet, click the Open button on the toolbar. In the resulting dialog box, select the name of the document you want to print, and click OK to open it.

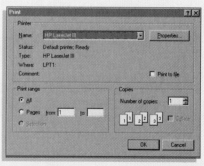

⑤ The resulting Print dialog box gives you several important options. For example, you can print the entire document or a specified range of pages; you can instruct WordPad to print multiple copies of your document; and you can choose to collate the copies or not. (Some options in the Print dialog box may be dimmed if they are not available for your printer.) Make any appropriate selections, and click OK to begin printing.

TIP SHEET

▶ **If you want to print only a particular passage from your document, begin by using the mouse or keyboard to select the text you want to print. Then choose Print from the File menu and click the Selection option in the Print dialog box. Click OK to begin printing.**

▶ **Optionally, click the Properties button on the Print dialog box to view or change the settings for your printer. The resulting dialog box shows an assortment of available printing options.**

▶ **See "How to Change the WordPad Settings" in Chapter 14 for more information about printing options in the WordPad application.**

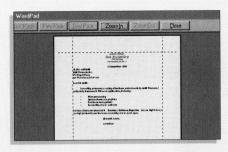

2 Optionally, click the Print Preview button on the toolbar to see what your document will look like when you print it.

3 In the preview window, examine your document and make sure it's formatted just the way you want it. Then click the Close button to return to the normal view of your document.

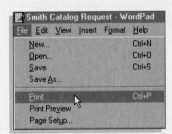

4 To print a single copy of your document under the default settings, click the Print button on the toolbar; WordPad immediately sends your document to the printer. Alternatively, to change the print settings, pull down the file menu and choose the Print command.

Janet Doe
Doe Accounting
123 Pear Street
San Francisco, CA 94114

15 September 1995

Mr. Maxwell Smith
Smith Products, Inc.
573 Roger Road
San Francisco, CA 94102

Dear Mr. Smith:

I am writing to request a catalog of business software sold by Smith Products, Inc. I am particularly interested in Windows applications, including:

- Word processing
- Spreadsheets and graphics
- Database management
- Accounting and tax software

I've read about your products in *Business Software Magazine*. As you might know, the editors had high praise for your low-cost accounting and tax packages.

Sincerely yours,

Janet Doe

TRY IT!

Here's a chance to review the word processing procedures you learned in the previous chapter. In the steps ahead you'll create the business letter shown below. You'll type the text of the document first, and then go back and reformat it. In the final steps you'll save the document to disk and print it on paper.

Click the Start button and choose Programs. Choose Accessories from the Programs menu and then choose WordPad from the Accessories menu.

Smith Products, Inc.
573 Roger Road
San Francisco, CA 94102

18 September 1995

Ms. Janet Doe
Doe Accounting
123 Pear Street
San Francisco, CA 94114

Dear Ms. Doe:

Thank you for your interest in our business applications for Windows. As you look through our latest catalog, you'll find three great Fall promotions:

- 15% off the regular price of our popular DoTax program
- Our snappy new DoChart program introduced at only $19.95
- A free copy of our new ScreenSaver collection with any purchase

Business Software Magazine will be running another review of our products in the next issue. I hope you see it.

Sincerely yours,

Maxwell Smith

2

Click the Maximize button at the upper-right corner of the WordPad window.

3

Type **Smith Products, Inc.** and then press Enter.

4

Type the remaining two lines of the return address, pressing Enter after each line.

5

Press Enter again to insert a blank line. Then type the date and press Enter twice.

6

Type the four lines of the inside address, pressing Enter after each line.

7

Press Enter, type **Dear Ms. Doe:** and press Enter twice.

8

Press the Tab key to indent, and then type the entire first paragraph of the letter. Remember, do not press Enter to start new lines within the paragraph. At the end of the paragraph, press Enter twice.

9

Click the Bullets button on the toolbar, and then type the three lines of the bulleted list. After the last line, press Enter and then click the Bullets button again to turn off bulleting. Press Enter to insert a blank line.

Continue to next page ▶

TRY IT!

Continue
below

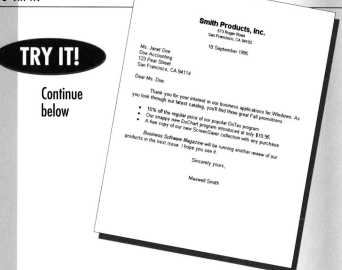

10

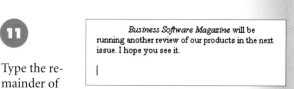

Press Tab to indent the second paragraph. Click the Italics button on the toolbar so that the next text you type will be in italics. Type *Business Software Magazine* and then click the Italics button again to turn italics off.

11

> *Business Software Magazine* will be running another review of our products in the next issue. I hope you see it.
>
> |

Type the remainder of the second paragraph in regular (nonitalic) text. Press Enter twice at the end of the paragraph.

12

> Sincerely yours,
>
> Maxwell Smith|

Press Tab four times and type **Sincerely yours,**. Then press Enter four times. Press Tab four times again, and then type **Maxwell Smith**. You've now finished typing the letter.

13

> Smith Products, Inc.
> 573 Roger Road
> San Francisco, CA 94102

Press Ctrl+Home to move to the top of the document, and use your mouse to select the first line of text.

14

Click the Bold button on the format bar to apply the boldface style to the text.

15

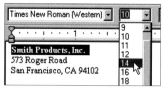

Pull down the Size list on the format bar, and choose 14 as the new size of the selected text.

16

Select the two lines of the return address, pull down the Size list, and choose 8 as the new size of these lines.

Use your mouse to select the company name, the return address, and the date.

Click the Center button on the format bar to center the lines you've selected.

Press Ctrl+A to select the entire text of the document.

Pull down the Font list on the format bar and choose Arial as the new font for the document.

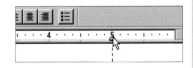

With the entire document still selected, drag the right indent marker to the 5-inch measurement along the Ruler.

Select the three lines of the bulleted list and drag the square left indent marker to the ½-inch measurement along the Ruler.

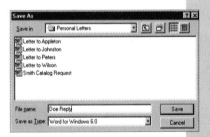

Click the Save button on the toolbar. Type **Doe Reply** as the file name and click OK.

Click the Print button on the toolbar to print the letter.

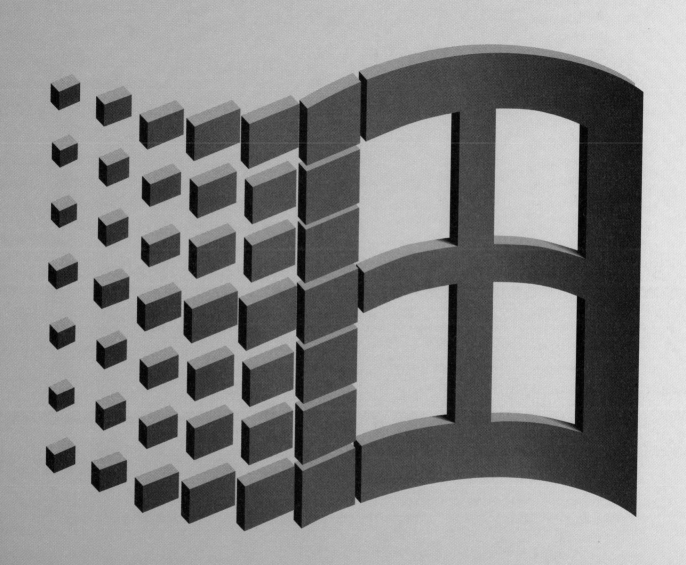

CHAPTER 8

Using the Clipboard

In Windows 95 you can freely transfer information from one place to another on the desktop. For example, during a typical Windows session you might move a paragraph from the middle to the beginning of a WordPad document or copy a block of text from one word processed document to another. Later, you might decide to copy a selection of financial data from your spreadsheet program to a memo you're preparing in WordPad or even move a graphic image from the Paint program to your memo.

All these procedures make use of the Clipboard, an intermediate storage facility for information you're moving or copying from one place to another in Windows. Any time you transfer information—whether the operation involves a single document, two documents within the same program, or two different applications—Windows automatically places the information in the Clipboard.

Simple Clipboard transfers are known as cut-and-paste and copy-and-paste operations. In this chapter you'll learn how to copy and move information in Windows, via the Clipboard. You'll also find out how to use the Clipboard to capture screen images from the desktop and copy them to any document you're creating. Chapter 15 describes and illustrates a more advanced kind of data transfer known as Object Linking and Embedding, or OLE.

How to Copy and Paste

To copy information from one place to another in Windows you use the copy-and-paste procedure. Ctrl+C is the standard keyboard shortcut for the Copy command, and Ctrl+V is the shortcut for the Paste command. To carry out a copy-and-paste procedure you begin by selecting a block of information at its source and copying it to the Clipboard; then you select a destination and paste the information from the Clipboard. You can copy information within a single document, or from one document to another on the desktop.

▶ **①** To copy information from one place to another within a single document, begin by selecting the information you want to copy. Although some applications have their own special selection techniques, you can generally use either the mouse or the keyboard to select information: Drag the mouse from the beginning to the end of the selection, or hold down the Shift key and use the arrow keys to select the information. The selected material is highlighted.

⑥ To copy information from a file in one application to a document in another application, begin by selecting the information in the source location. Press Ctrl+C to copy the selection to the Clipboard. Start the second application and open the document to which you want to copy the information. Select the location where you want the copy to appear, and press Ctrl+V to paste the information from the Clipboard.

TIP SHEET

▶ The central graphic on these pages illustrates a copy-and-paste operation from a Paint file to a WordPad document. See Chapter 13 for an introduction to the Paint program.

▶ When you're copying from one application to another, you may want to view both the source and destination applications on the desktop at once, as shown here in the central graphic. To review the techniques for arranging windows, see "How to Arrange Windows on the Desktop" in Chapter 2.

▶ To view the current contents of the Clipboard, choose Clipboard Viewer from the Accessories list in the Start menu.

2 Hold down the Ctrl key and press C to copy the selection to the Clipboard.

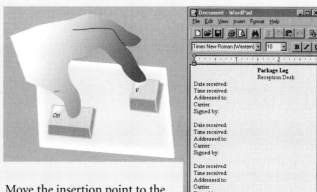

3 Move the insertion point to the location where you want the information to appear. Then hold down the Ctrl key and press V. If you want to make additional copies, repeat this step.

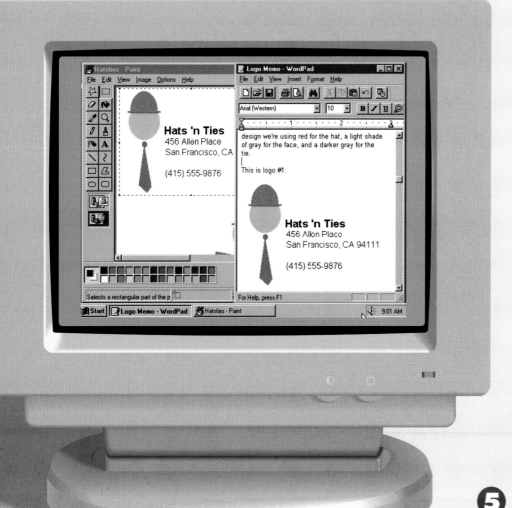

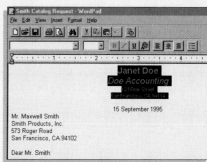

4 To copy information from one document to another within an application, first select the information and press Ctrl+C, just as you would do to copy information within a single document.

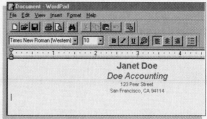

5 Open the destination document and select the location where you want to insert the copy. Press Ctrl+V to paste the information from the Clipboard.

How to Cut and Paste

To move information in Windows you use the cut-and-paste procedure, which deletes information from its source and places it in a new location. In any application that allows cut-and-paste, the Edit menu contains Cut and Paste commands with standard keyboard shortcuts of Ctrl+X and Ctrl+V, respectively. Like copy-and-paste, this procedure has two basic steps: You begin by selecting a block of information at its source and "cutting" it to the Clipboard; then you select a destination and paste the information from the Clipboard. Probably the most common use of the cut-and-paste operation is to move information within one document.

▶ **1** Select the information you want to move. You can generally use either the mouse or the keyboard to select information: Drag the mouse from the beginning to the end of the selection, or hold down the Shift key and use the arrow keys to highlight the selection. In this example the selection is a short paragraph near the end of a memo written in WordPad. The goal is to move the text to a new position just after the first paragraph of the document.

TIP SHEET

▶ **You can paste multiple copies by pressing Ctrl+V more than once.**

▶ **If you cut information from a document and then change your mind about the operation, pull down the Edit menu and choose Undo.**

▶ **The WordPad application provides a second convenient technique for moving text from one place to another in a document: Select the target text, and then use your mouse to *drag* the text from its source to the new location. Your choice between these two techniques will depend on the length of your document, the amount of text you want to move, and the distance of the move. (See "How to Use Text Shortcuts" in Chapter 14 for more information.)**

2 Hold down the Ctrl key and press X to cut the selection to the Clipboard. The selection immediately disappears from its original location.

3 Select the location to which you want to move the information. (In WordPad, move the insertion point to the destination.)

Memo

To:	All Managers
From:	J.J.
Re:	New Store Logo

We've finally settled on two candidates for our new logo. Our goalwas to produce a simple, whimsical design that would work successfully in a variety of promotional materials. In each design we're using red for the hat, a light shade of gray for the face, and a darker gray for the tie.

Take a look at both candidates and let me know which one you prefer. We want to make a decision by the end of the week.

This is logo #1:

Hats 'n Ties
456 Allen Place
San Francisco, CA 94111

(415) 555-9876

And this is logo #2:

Hats 'n Ties
456 Allen Place
San Francisco, CA 94111

(415) 555-9876

Thanks,
J.J.

This paragraph was moved here from the end of the document.

4 Hold down the Ctrl key and press V to paste the selection from the Clipboard to its new location.

How to Capture a Desktop Image

Occasionally you may want to capture the image of a window that appears on the desktop. For example, you can capture and print an application window so you can keep notes about using particular features in the program. Or, you might want to capture the image of a folder as a way of keeping track of the files you've saved in the folder. When you capture a desktop image, Windows stores it in the Clipboard. From there, you can copy the image to a WordPad document or any other file that can include graphic inserts.

▶ ❶ Open the window that you want to capture as a desktop image. You can capture any window on the desktop, regardless of the window's contents.

TIP SHEET

▶ **You can capture an image of the entire desktop by pressing the Print Screen key alone.**

▶ **Once you've pasted a captured image to a WordPad document, you can print a copy of the document on any printer that has graphics capabilities.**

▶ **Copy an image to the Paint program if you want to change the image in any way, or if you want to select and work with a portion of the image. See Chapter 13 for more information.**

❹ Press Ctrl+V to copy the captured image to the document.

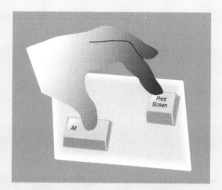

2 Hold down the Alt key and press the Print Screen key.

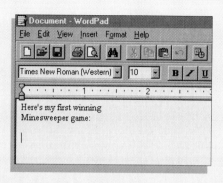

3 Open the document to which you want to copy the window image, and select the location where you want the image to appear.

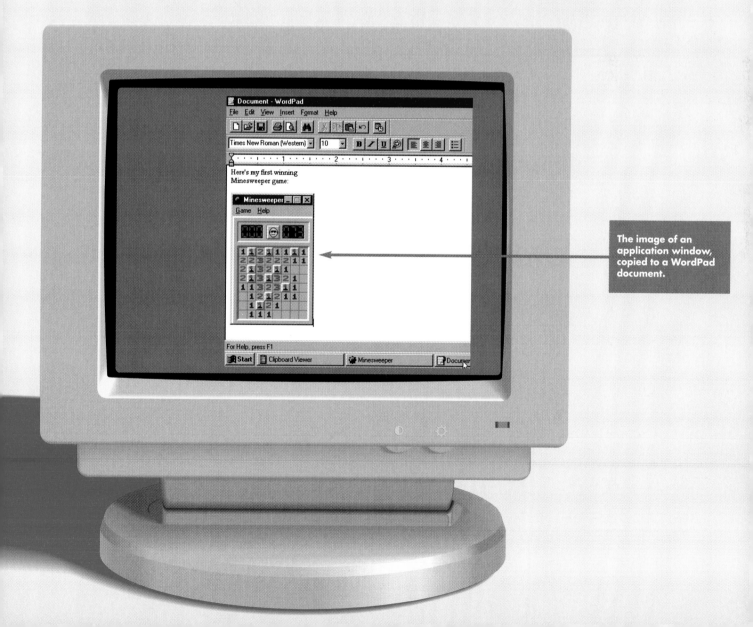

The image of an application window, copied to a WordPad document.

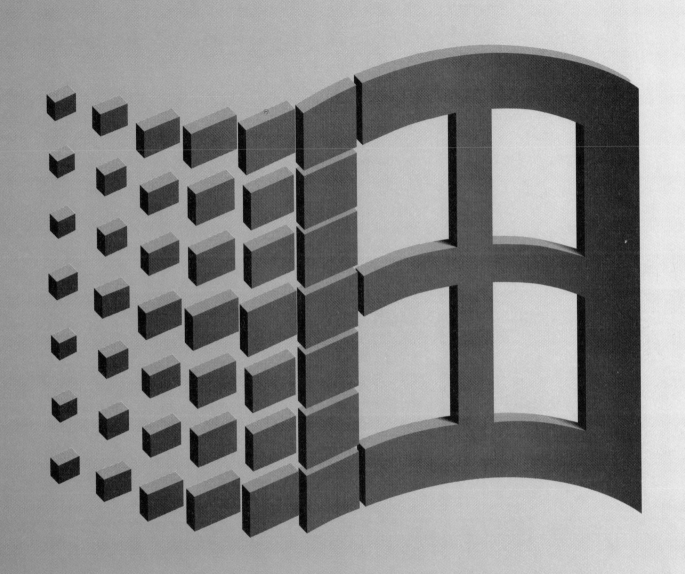

CHAPTER 9

Printing

When you print a document, Windows 95 coordinates the software resources needed for the job—including the printer driver, the font selections, and the contents of the document itself. All this takes place automatically, without distracting you from your other activities on the desktop. A printer icon shows up at the right side of the Taskbar whenever you choose an application's Print command. Windows allows you to place multiple documents in line for printing—creating a print queue—and to continue your work while the printing takes place in the background.

You may sometimes want to take more direct control over printing operations. One way to do so is to place a shortcut icon on the desktop to represent your printer. You can then form a *print queue* (a series of documents waiting to print) by dragging documents directly to the printer icon. To view the print queue, you simply double-click on the printer icon; in the resulting window you can issue commands to pause, resume, or cancel any print job.

You'll see how to perform all these tasks in this chapter. In addition, you'll learn how to install the driver for a newly connected printer when necessary.

How to Print a Document

You typically print a document directly from the application in which the file was originally created. Whether you're printing a letter from WordPad, a drawing from Paint, or a table of financial data from your favorite spreadsheet program, the steps are always the same: Start the application, open the file, edit it if necessary, and then choose the program's Print command to send the document to the printer. But suppose you want a quick way to print several documents from a variety of source applications. To simplify this kind of printing operation, you can create a shortcut icon to represent your printer on the desktop. You then use a simple drag-and-drop action to print a file.

TIP SHEET

▸ **You can drag multiple document files to the printer icon in one operation. To select two or more files, hold down the Ctrl key while you click the file names in the source folder window. Then drag the entire selection to the printer shortcut icon.**

▸ **To view the current print queue, double-click the printer icon on the desktop. When you open the printer window, you can manage the queue in a variety of useful ways. Turn the page for more information.**

▸ **If Windows can't automatically determine the application from which to print a document you select, the simplest solution is to start an appropriate application yourself, open the document, and choose the Print command from the application's File menu. A more technical alternative is to associate an application with a particular file type. To do so, open the My Computer window or the Explorer, pull down the View menu, and choose Options. Click the File Types tab to register a new file type.**

▶ **1** To open the Printers folder, click the Start button, choose Settings, and then choose Printers.

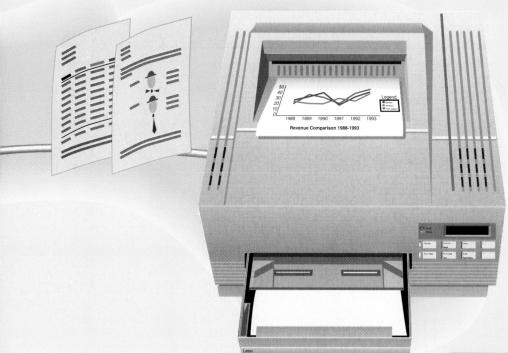

2 The Printers folder displays icons for the printers you've installed on your system. Select the printer for which you want to create a shortcut on the desktop.

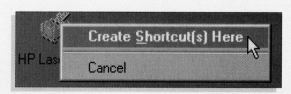

3 Holding down the right (or secondary) mouse button, drag the selected printer icon from the Printers folder to the desktop. Release the mouse button and then choose Create Shortcut(s) Here from the resulting menu. A new printer icon appears on the desktop, where it will remain until you delete it. You can now close the Printers folder.

4 Use the My Computer icon to open a folder containing one or more document files that you want to print.

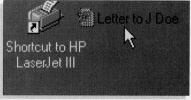

5 Drag any document from the open folder to the printer shortcut icon. Release the mouse button when the document icon is directly in front of the printer icon and the name of the printer is highlighted. In response, Windows starts the application in which the file was created, opens the document, prints it, and then closes the application.

6 If Windows displays an error message, the document you've selected is not associated with an application. Click OK to close the message box. See the Tip Sheet for solutions to this problem.

How to Manage the Print Queue

The print queue is the list of documents waiting to be printed. You can open a window that displays this queue by double-clicking the printer shortcut icon you've created on the desktop. This window allows you to pause the current print operation, either for the entire queue or for individual documents in the queue. You can also cancel any job in the queue.

▶ **1** Click the printer shortcut icon with the right (or secondary) mouse button, and choose Pause Printing from the resulting menu. When you have several documents to send to the print queue, the Pause status gives you the opportunity to form the entire queue before the printing begins.

6 To remove a document from the print queue, click a document name with the right (or secondary) mouse button, and choose the Cancel Printing command. The name of the document will disappear from the queue and the document will not be printed.

5 To resume printing any documents that are not in the Pause mode, pull down the Printer menu and choose the Pause Printing option. (The check mark next to this option means that the entire queue is in the Pause mode. When you choose the command, the check mark is removed and printing resumes.)

2 Send any number of documents to the printer, using the drag-and-drop operation described on the previous two pages.

4 To change the status of any document in the list, click the document name with the right (or secondary) mouse button. Then choose the Pause Printing option to toggle the document into the Pause mode.

3 To view the print queue, double-click the printer shortcut icon on the desktop. The queue shows the name of each document that's waiting to be printed.

How to Install a Printer

From time to time you may want to connect a different printer to your computer. To work successfully with a newly attached printer, you have to install an important piece of software known as a driver. Windows 95 comes with a large collection of drivers for the most popular printers on the market today. The Add Printer Wizard helps you select and install the appropriate driver for your printer.

TIP SHEET

▶ **When two or more printers are installed, the** *default* **printer is the one that's automatically used for printing applications unless you specify otherwise. To change the default printer, open the Printers folder and select a printer. Then pull down the File menu and choose the Set As Default command.**

▶ **If you're installing a printer that you've just purchased, the package may include a driver disk. When you reach step 3, insert the driver disk in the appropriate drive, and click the Have Disk button. Windows will install the driver for you.**

▶ **Printer manufacturers periodically update their driver software and make the new versions available to registered printer owners. You may be able to request the new version by phone or download it from your favorite online service.**

1 Click the Start button and choose Settings. Then choose Printers to open the Printers folder.

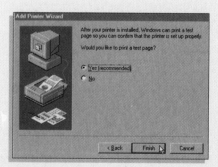

6 In the next window, indicate whether or not you want Windows to print a test page on your printer. (If your printer isn't actually attached yet, select No.) When you click the Finish button, the Wizard instructs you to insert the appropriate Windows installation disk into your disk drive. Windows copies the necessary printer driver from this disk to your hard disk to complete the installation process.

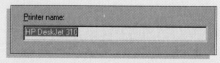

5 Click Next again to accept the suggested printer name. This will be the name of the printer icon that Windows adds to your Printers folder.

2 Double-click the Add Printer icon in the Printers folder. The first window of the Add Printer Wizard appears on the desktop, as shown in the central graphic on these pages. Click the Next button to begin the process of installing a new printer. (If you are installed on a network, the Printer Wizard next asks you if this is a local or network printer. Select the appropriate option and click Next.)

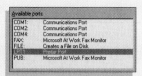

4 Select the name of the port where the printer is attached. In most cases, this name is LPT1:, the Printer Port. Click Next to continue.

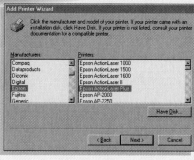

3 In the next window, select the manufacturer of your printer. Then select the printer model you want to install. Click Next to continue.

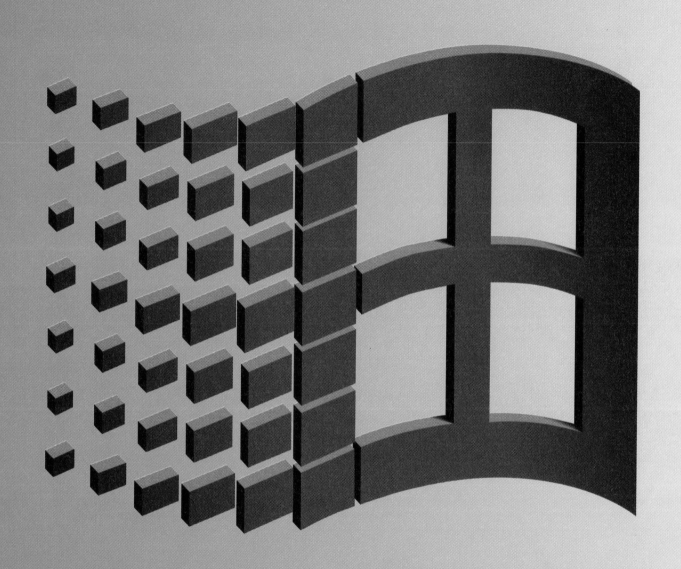

CHAPTER 10

Using Other Applications

 Along with popular applications such as the WordPad word processing program and the Paint drawing program, Windows 95 provides several additional tools that you may want to run from time to time. This chapter is a brief look at two other programs you're likely to find useful.

Calculator gives you the equivalent of a multifunction hand-held calculator. You can use this program for quick calculations, and you can copy the results to other applications via the Clipboard.

Notepad is a text editor, useful for creating and editing data files, program listings, or system files.

How to Use the Calculator

With the Calculator program open on your desktop, you can perform quick arithmetic operations or find the results of complex mathematical functions simply by clicking buttons with the mouse. For convenience, the application window appears in two versions; the one you choose depends on the complexity of the calculations you need to perform. A standard ten-key calculator provides the familiar arithmetic operations. A more elaborate scientific calculator has several columns of advanced mathematical functions.

TIP SHEET

▶ The scientific calculator has an additional memory device called the Statistics Box, in which you can temporarily store a sequence of numeric values. To open this box, click the Sta button at the left side of the application window. Arrange your desktop so you can see the Calculator window and Statistics Box at the same time. To copy a number into the box, enter the value in the Calculator's display area, and then click the Dat button; repeat this process for additional values. To perform statistical operations on the values currently in the box, click Sum for the total of all the numbers, Ave for the average, or s for the standard deviation.

▶ The scientific calculator also gives you a quick way to find the hexadecimal, octal, or binary equivalent of a decimal number. Enter the value into the display area, and then click one of the number-base option buttons—Hex, Oct, or Bin.

▶ To close the Calculator program, click the Close button at the upper-right corner of the window.

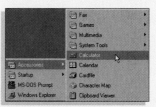

▶ **1** To start the Calculator, click the Start button and choose Programs. Then choose Accessories and click Calculator.

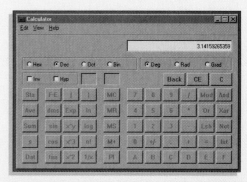

6 To view the scientific calculator, pull down the View menu and click Scientific. The various function keys are arranged on either side of the number buttons.

2 Try performing an operation, just as you would on a hand-held calculator: Click a sequence of digits with the mouse, or type them from the keyboard. (To use the numeric keypad, activate the Num Lock key.) Select an operator (+, -, *, or /) and then enter a second number. Click the = button to calculate the result.

3 Try another calculation, and experiment with the clear buttons. Click the Back button (or press Backspace) to erase the last digit you've typed. Click the CE button (or press Delete) to clear the most recent number you've entered. Click the C button (or press Escape) to clear an entire calculation.

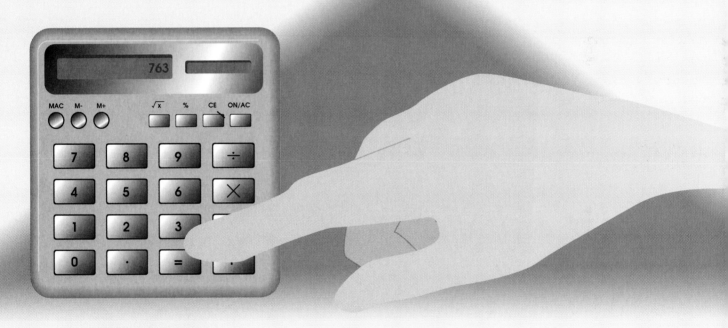

5 To copy the displayed value to the Clipboard, pull down the Edit menu and click Copy, or press Ctrl+C. You can then switch to another application and paste the result into a document. Switch back to the Calculator program when you're ready to resume your work.

4 The memory buttons allow you to store and reuse intermediate results in a multistep calculation. Click MS to store the current value in memory. Click MR to copy the contents of memory to the display area, where the value can be used in the current operation. Click M+ to add the currently displayed number to the value already in memory. Click MC to clear the memory. (Note that only one value can be stored in memory at a time. An M appears in the small box below the display area when there is a value in memory.)

How to Use the Notepad

In the Notepad application you can read, edit, or create files that consist solely of text. Here the word *text* generally refers to a sequence of characters that you type directly from the keyboard—uppercase and lowercase letters of the alphabet, digits from 0 to 9, punctuation, and other symbols such as #, @, and *. Notepad files do *not* contain the formatting and typographical information typical of word processed files. This distinction is important: If you want to create a document that may include fonts, typographical effects, paragraph formats, and graphics, use WordPad or another word processing program. If you want to read or create a file that contains only lines of unformatted text, Notepad is the right choice.

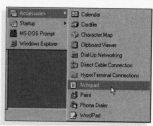

▶ **1** To open the Notepad application, click the Start menu and choose Programs. Then choose Accessories and click Notepad. When the program first appears on the desktop, the work area is empty except for a flashing vertical cursor.

6 If your text file contains long individual lines of text, pull down the Edit menu and choose the Word Wrap command. Notepad then breaks the text into smaller lines that you can view within the dimensions of the application window. This option affects only the display of your text; no actual line break is added to your file unless you press the Enter key.

TIP SHEET

▶ **To enter the current time and date into a text file, pull down the Edit menu and click the Time/Date command, or press F5.**

▶ **The Search menu contains commands that allow you to find specific sequences of text in an open Notepad file. Choose the Find command and enter the text you want to search for. Then click the Find Next button one or more times to search for all the occurrences of the target text in the file.**

2 To open an existing text file from disk, pull down the File menu and choose Open. Open the folder in which the file is located. Then select or type the name of the file you want to open, and click the Open button.

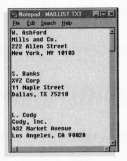

3 The text of the file appears in the work area. You can now revise the text in any way. For example, you can delete characters by positioning the cursor and pressing Backspace (to delete characters before the cursor) or Delete (to delete characters after the cursor). Insert new lines by moving the cursor to the end of an existing line and pressing Enter.

4 To save the changes you've made, pull down the File menu and choose Save. To print a copy of the current file, choose Print from the File menu.

5 To clear the current file from the Notepad window and start a new file, pull down the File menu and choose New. You can then begin typing new lines of text. Press Enter at the end of each line.

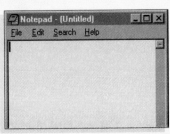

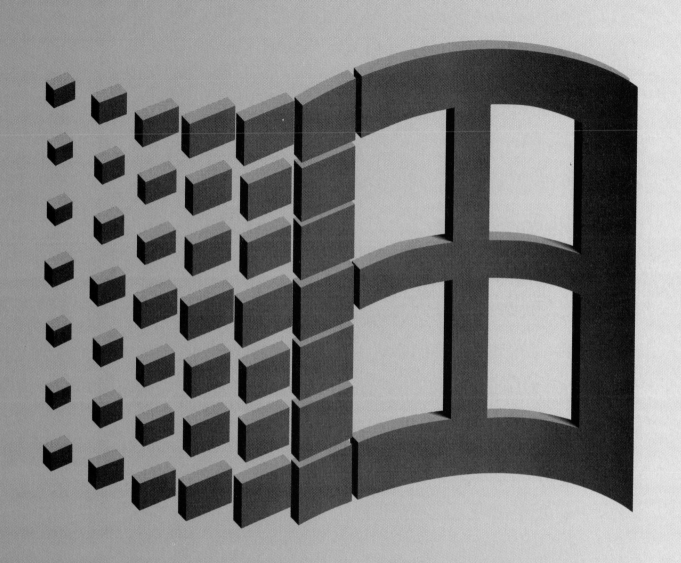

CHAPTER 11

Using Applications from Windows 3.1

 Even though Windows 95 is your new operating environment, you don't have to abandon the comfortable old programs that you used in Windows 3.1. In fact, if you installed Windows 95 *over* Windows 3.1 (copying the new system into the same directory as the old one) you can still run all the programs that were available to you before. In this chapter you'll take a look at two programs that were originally supplied as part of Windows 3.1, but can still be used profitably in Windows 95: Cardfile and Calendar.

Cardfile is a simple tool for storing and retrieving data records. What kinds of information do you regularly gather and use at work or at home? Addresses and phone numbers, to be sure—but also customer lists, investment ideas, household insurance inventories, research notes, holiday lists, New Year's resolutions, birthdays and anniversaries, cake recipes, vacation plans, kids' inoculation records, garden planting schedules—the list goes on and on and is as diverse as life is busy. Whether you've previously kept these records stored neatly in folders or scrawled on the backs of envelopes, you can significantly improve your access to information by organizing it in the Cardfile program.

The Calendar application provides a simple environment for keeping track of appointments. Staff meetings, business lunches, professional conferences, consultations, seminars, due dates, interviews, rendezvous, or mere tête-à-têtes—whatever your appointments and obligations are, you can use Calendar to schedule them and remind yourself when it is time to keep them.

How to Use Cardfile

A card is the space where you store one record of information in Cardfile. You can add many cards to a file. Each card contains an index line at the top, where you enter the title, topic, or primary data item of a particular record. In the information area, just below the index line, you type additional information. As you add new cards to a file, the program automatically arranges them in alphabetical order by the contents of their index lines. As you'll see, the steps for filling in the first card in a new file are a little different from those for adding subsequent cards.

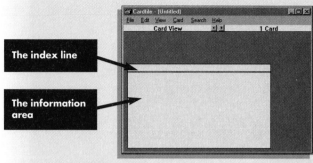

The index line

The information area

▶ **1** If Cardfile appears in your Accessories list, run the application by clicking the Start button choosing the program directly from the menu. Alternatively, choose Run from the Start menu, enter Cardfile in the Open box, and click OK. The Cardfile window appears on the desktop with a single empty card, ready for your first record entry.

TIP SHEET

▶ **To view a list of all the index lines in your current file, choose the List command from the View menu. You can select any entry in this list and then choose the Card command from the View menu to view the corresponding card.**

▶ **Another quick way to go to a card is to choose Go To from the Search menu or press F4. In the Go To dialog box, enter any part of the index-line text that you want to search for and click OK. Cardfile instantly moves the corresponding card to the front of the file.**

▶ **To delete a card, move the card to the front of the file and choose Delete from the Card menu. Click OK to confirm. To duplicate a card, move the card to the front and choose Duplicate from the Card menu. This is a quick way to create a new card from information contained in an existing card. Double-click the index line of the duplicate to create a unique index for the new card.**

▶ **You can create any number of card files and save them on disk under unique names. To open a particular file, choose the Open command from the File menu when you first start the Cardfile program.**

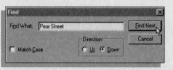

7 To search for information in your file, pull down the Search menu and choose Find. In the Find What box, enter the information you want to search for and then click Find Next. The program searches for the target text in the information area of your current cards. If the text is found, the card that contains it is moved to the front of the file. Press F3 to search for the same text in other cards.

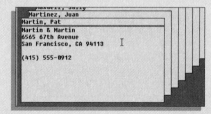

6 To view a particular card, click its index line, or press PgUp or PgDn repeatedly until the card you want to see appears in the front of the stack. If necessary, you can edit the front card by typing new text in its information area.

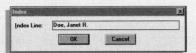

2 To create the index for your first record, double-click the index line or press F6. In the resulting Index box, enter a line of text to identify your first record. For example, if you are developing an address file, enter the name a person whose address you want to store in the file. Press Enter or click OK to confirm the index entry. The text appears on the index line in the first card, and a flashing cursor appears at the top of the information area.

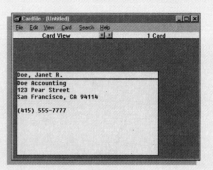

3 Now type the information you want to store in this card. The card contains room for eleven 40-character lines of text, which you can organize in any way you want. Word wrap takes place when you reach the end of a line. Alternatively, you can press Enter to start a new line.

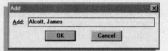

4 When you're ready to add the next card to your file, pull down the Card menu and choose Add, or simply press F7. In the Add dialog box, enter an index line for the new card. (Remember to enter the same type of information for every new card in your file. For example, enter the name of a person, an inventory item, or a research topic.) Press Enter or click OK to confirm the index entry. Then complete the new card by typing lines of text into the information area.

5 Repeat step 4 for each card you want to add to the file. To save your file to disk, pull down the File menu, choose Save As, and enter a name for the file. Click OK to complete the Save operation. As you continue adding new cards, you'll want to update your file from time to time by choosing Save from the File menu.

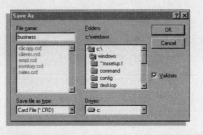

How to Use Calendar

When you first start the Calendar application, you see a blank appointment sheet for today's date. You create your own personal calendar file by selecting among the available customization options and then saving the file to disk. Over time, you'll keep all your appointments in this one file. You can enter appointments and reminders for any date in the future, or notes about events that took place in the past. For your most important dates you can even set an alarm.

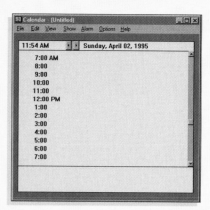

▶ **1** If Calendar appears in your Accessories list, run the application by clicking the Start button and choosing the program directly from the menu. Alternatively, choose Run from the Start file, enter Calendar in the Open box, and click OK. The Calendar window appears on the desktop with a blank sheet for today's date. By scrolling through the sheet, you'll see that it includes an appointment line for every hour of the day, from midnight to 11 p.m.

The scratch pad

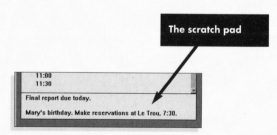

7 In addition to the appointment lines themselves, each date sheet has a scratch pad where you can enter notes and reminders that apply to the entire day. Press Tab to activate the scratch pad, and type as many as three lines of text.

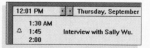

6 To set an alarm, click the time when you want the alarm to sound and press F5 (or choose Set from the Alarm menu). A bell icon appears to the left of the time entry. When an alarm goes off, you'll hear four beeps and you'll see a reminder message on the desktop.

2 Before creating your personal calendar file, you can customize the appointment sheet if you wish. Pull down the Options menu and choose Day Settings. In the resulting dialog box, you can change three characteristics of the sheet: the time interval between appointment lines, the time format (12-hour or 24-hour), and the time that initially appears at the top of the sheet. Make any changes you want in these options, and click OK.

3 Now pull down the File menu and choose Save As. Enter a name for your personal calendar file and click OK. As you begin entering appointments, you can update your file at any time by choosing the Save command from the File menu.

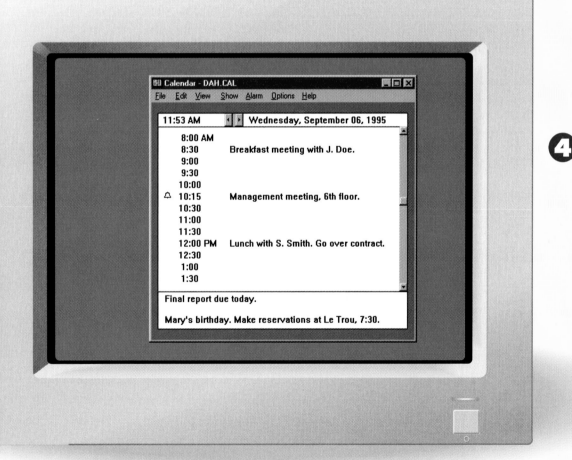

4 To enter an appointment, begin by selecting the correct date and time. Click the right or left arrow on the *status line* to scroll to a different day. (Alternatively, press Ctrl+PgUp to move to a date in the past or Ctrl+PgDn to move to a date in the future.) In the appropriate date sheet, use the arrow keys on the keyboard to move the cursor to the time of your appointment. Then type your appointment. Each line on a date sheet can hold up to 80 characters of text.

5 To create an appointment line for a time that doesn't appear in the regular intervals of your date sheet, pull down the Options menu and choose Special Time, or press F7. In the resulting dialog box, enter the time and click the Insert button. Back on the date sheet, type a line of text for this new time entry.

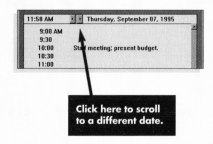

Click here to scroll to a different date.

CHAPTER 12

Playing Games

 After a stretch of serious computer activity, a game program provides a calming and salutary break from your work. Play a couple of hands of cards or solve a challenging puzzle on the computer screen; you'll return to your work with a fresh point of view and an alert mind.

In Windows 95 you'll find some classic games along with a few new ones. Solitaire is a fast-moving version of everyone's favorite one-person card game. The computer shuffles and deals the cards for you and sets up the playing table; you move quickly through the game by dragging and clicking your cards with the mouse. Other enticing card games include Hearts and FreeCell. By contrast, Minesweeper is an entertaining test of logical skills and deductive powers.

If these games aren't currently available on your computer, you can install them by double-clicking the Add/Remove Programs icon in the Control Panel and then clicking the Windows Setup tab. See "How to Add Windows Components" in Chapter 16 for further details. One caveat, however: Some employers fail to understand the therapeutic value in an occasional break from work. If your boss is looking over your shoulder and expecting to see a budget spreadsheet or a sales report, you may want to postpone your next round of Minesweeper for another time.

How to Play Card Games

The Games menu in the Accessories list has a variety of card games for you to choose from, including FreeCell, Hearts, and the ever popular Solitaire. After starting a round in any of these games, you can minimize the program window whenever you need to turn your attention to some other activity. To continue to your game later, just click the program's button on the taskbar.

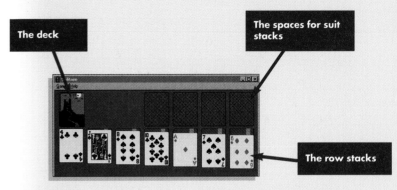

The deck

The spaces for suit stacks

The row stacks

TIP SHEET

▶ **FreeCell is another card game that you play alone. The object is to move all 52 cards in suit order to the "home cells" at the upper-right corner of the play area. The strategy is more demanding in FreeCell than in Solitaire.**

▶ **Unlike Solitaire and FreeCell, the Hearts game takes four players. The object is to finish the game with the *lowest* score. To achieve this, you try to avoid capturing any "trick" containing heart cards or the queen of spades. If you play against the computer, the hands of the three other players are managed by the Hearts program itself; alternatively, you can sign on to the Microsoft Hearts network to compete against real players.**

▶ **To find out more about any of these games, start the program of your choice, pull down the Help menu in the game window, and choose Help Topics.**

1 To play Solitaire, choose Games from the Accessories list, and then choose the Solitaire program from the resulting menu. The program deals seven "row stacks" and leaves the remainder of the deck face-down at the upper-left corner of the window. You'll eventually build "suit stacks" in the four spaces at the upper-right corner. A suit stack is a sequence of cards in a given suit, arranged in ascending order from ace to king. The object of the game is to move all 52 cards to their respective suit stacks.

6 To change the way the next game is played or scored, choose Options from the Game menu. In the resulting dialog box you can specify the number of cards that will be turned over each time you draw from the deck and you can select a scoring system. You can also activate a timed game.

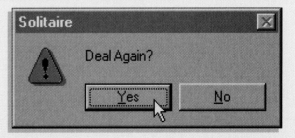

5 You win if you manage to arrange all 52 cards in their respective suit stacks. In response, the cards begin an animated cascade down the screen. Press any key to stop the animation, and then click Yes to start a new game.

2 Begin rearranging the row stacks to create consecutive sequences of cards in descending order and in alternating colors. Use the mouse to drag a card from one stack to another. To turn over a face-down card in a row stack, click the card once. A king can be moved to an empty position in the row stacks. If you uncover an ace, you can move it to the suit stacks by dragging it up or simply by double-clicking the card; then you can continue moving consecutive cards to the suit stack.

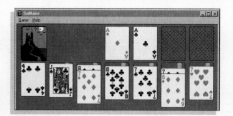

3 When you can't move any more cards among the row stacks, click the top card in the deck to turn it over. Try to find a place for the new card, either in the row stacks or the suit stacks. Then click the deck again to view the next card.

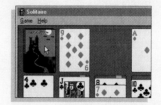

4 Continue until you've turned over the entire deck. Then prepare to go through the deck another time, if necessary, by clicking the blank space at the upper-left corner of the window.

Click here to go through the deck again.

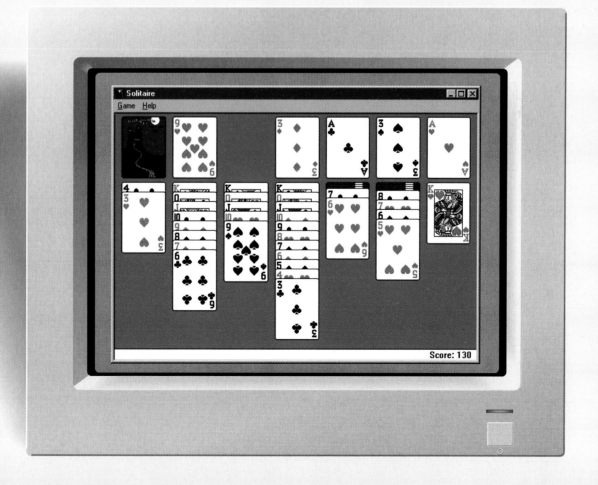

How to Play Minesweeper

In Minesweeper, the game window is a field of mines that you have to identify and mark in the best time possible. The field is divided into squares. As you uncover each square, you may find a number that tells you how many mines exist in the surrounding squares. (A blank square has no surrounding mines.) If you uncover a mine, you lose the game. You win by successfully uncovering all the squares that do not contain mines, and correctly marking all the squares that do. As you master this game, you can advance through three levels of play—beginning, intermediate, and expert.

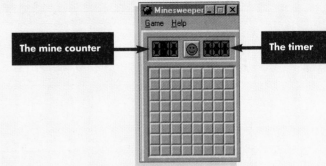

The mine counter

The timer

▶ **1** To start Minesweeper, choose the program from the Games menu in the Accessories list. When you play the game for the first time, the field is an eight-by-eight grid of squares. A counter at the upper-left corner of the game window shows you the number of mines you have to find; the timer at the upper-right corner shows the number of seconds you've been playing.

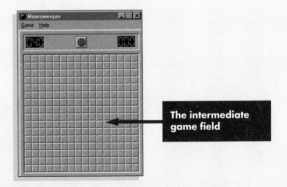

The intermediate game field

5 To try a new level, pull down the Game menu and click Intermediate or Expert. The higher the level, the larger the game field and the more mines there are to mark.

TIP SHEET

▶ Minesweeper keeps track of your best playing times at each game level. To see the recorded times, pull down the Game menu and choose Best Times.

▶ For additional tips and hints about the strategy of the Minesweeper game, pull down the Help menu and choose Help Topics.

2 To uncover a square, click it with the left mouse button. To mark a mine, click it with the right mouse button.

3 You win the game when you successfully mark all the mines and uncover all un-mined squares.

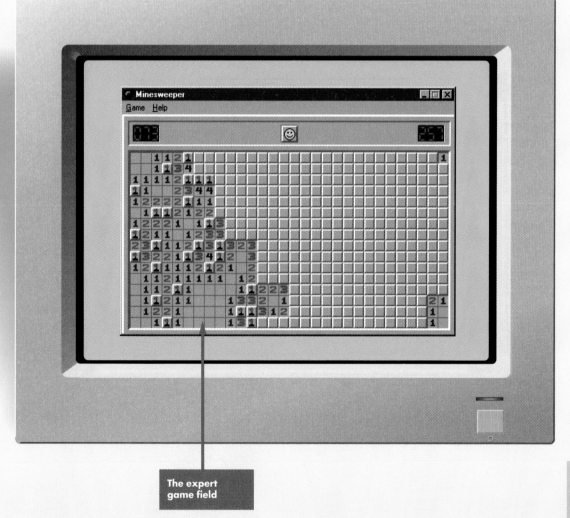

The expert game field

4 If you uncover a mine, the game is over. The program reveals all the mine locations. To start a new game, click the yellow face between the two counters at the top of the window.

Click here for a new game.

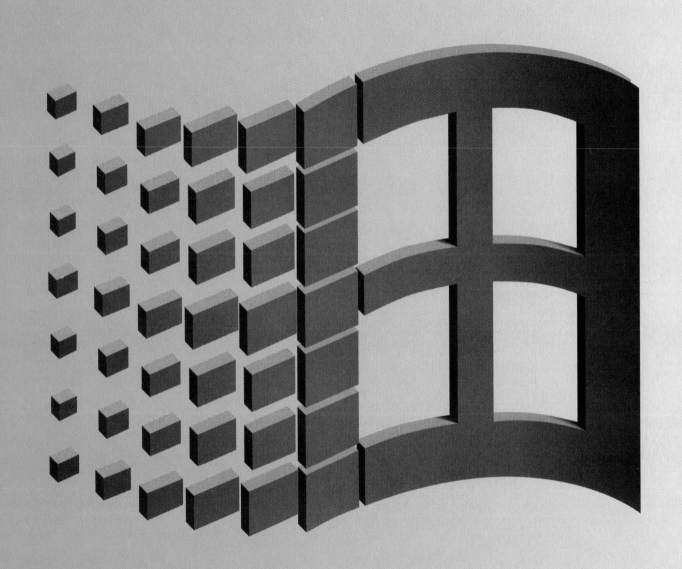

CHAPTER 13

Creating Artwork

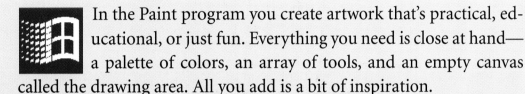 In the Paint program you create artwork that's practical, educational, or just fun. Everything you need is close at hand— a palette of colors, an array of tools, and an empty canvas called the drawing area. All you add is a bit of inspiration.

To begin a Paint picture, you select a tool and start drawing with the mouse. Some of the tools are for freehand sketching, while others are designed to help you create perfectly formed shapes such as lines, curves, rectangles, circles, ovals, and multisided figures. With a special feature called a cutout you move shapes around the canvas or duplicate any part of your drawing. You can even add text to your work. If you make a mistake, you use an eraser to remove it—or you can clear the canvas in an instant to start all over again.

What you do with all these tools and colors is up to you. Whether you're drawing a map to your house, decorating a birthday invitation, or designing a corporate logo, Paint provides an engaging medium for your creative efforts.

How to Get Started in Paint

When you start the Paint program, you'll find an assortment of tools and color choices arranged conveniently around the perimeter of a large drawing area. You use the mouse for two main purposes—first to select appropriate tools and then to draw pictures. When you click a drawing tool—the brush or the pencil tool, for example—the mouse in effect *becomes* that tool in the drawing area. In the steps ahead you'll begin exploring the many features of the Paint program.

▶ ① Click the Start button and choose Programs. Choose Accessories from the Programs menu, and click Paint to start the application. Maximize the Paint window to make as much room for your work as possible.

⑦ To erase your squiggle and start again with an empty drawing area, pull down the File menu and choose New (or simply press Ctrl+N). Paint asks you if you want to save the changes in the current drawing. Click the No button.

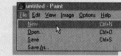

⑥ Hold down the left mouse button and drag the mouse to draw a squiggle on the screen. Release the mouse button when you're done. Like the pencil, the brush is a freehand drawing tool that records the path of the mouse's motion. You'll try out other tools later in this chapter.

TIP SHEET

▶ **To save a drawing to disk, pull down the File menu and choose the Save As command. In the Save As dialog box, enter a name for the file and click OK. By default, Paint supplies a .BMP extension. Once you've named and saved a file for the first time, you can choose the Save command from the File menu (or press Ctrl+S) to update the file with the latest changes to your drawing.**

▶ **To open an existing .BMP file from disk, pull down the File menu and choose Open (or press Ctrl+O). Select a file name from the list and click OK.**

⑤ Move the mouse pointer into the *drawing area,* the large empty section of the Paint window. Here the pointer represents the current drawing tool. With the brush tool selected, the pointer appears as a small diagonal line enclosed within crosshair markers.

2 Move the mouse pointer into the *toolbox* at the left side of the window. The pointer becomes an arrow that you can use to select any of the available drawing tools. The pencil—a freehand tool for drawing lines—is the initial selection. Try clicking the brush tool, located just to the right of the pencil; a single click selects the new tool.

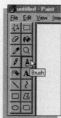

3 Move the mouse pointer down to the box located just beneath the toolbox. This box contains a variety of settings for the drawing tool you've selected. For the brush, the options represent different shapes and widths that the brush can produce in the drawing area. For this exercise, click the first diagonal line in the third row of shapes.

The toolbox

The drawing area

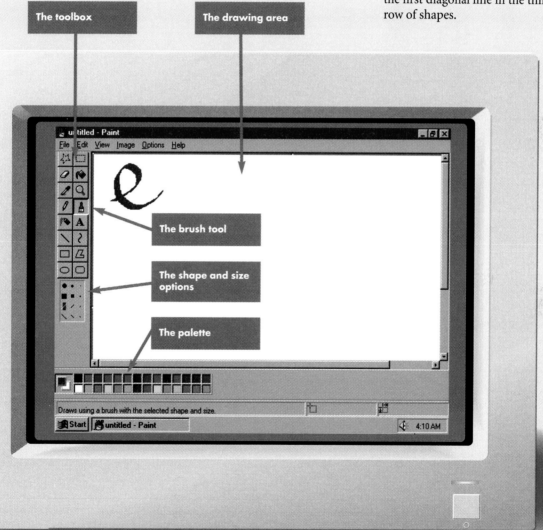

The brush tool

The shape and size options

The palette

4 Move down to the *palette*, the collection of colors you can use in your artwork. As you'll learn later, you can select foreground and background colors for your work. For now, use the left (or primary) mouse button to select blue from the middle of the lower row of colors.

How to Change Widths and Colors

To vary the effect of drawing tools in the Paint program, you can make selections from the box of options shown just below the toolbox. For example, suppose you're working with the brush tool. By clicking one of the settings displayed beneath the toolbox, you can change the size or shape of subsequent brush-strokes. Likewise, by selecting new colors in the palette, you change the brushstroke color. As you'll learn in the following steps, foreground and background color selections are made by clicking in the palette with the left and right mouse buttons.

1 Select the brush tool in the toolbox, and then click any of the width and shape settings displayed below the toolbox. A highlight marks the current selection.

▶ Paint uses both the left and right mouse buttons. By default, the *primary* button is the one on the left, and the *secondary* button is on the right. See "How to Change the Mouse Settings" in Chapter 4 for information about reversing the roles of the two buttons.

▶ To change the border width for a filled geometric shape (rectangle, oval, polygon, or rounded rectangle), first choose the line tool and change the width setting in the box shown below the toolbar. Then select the tool for drawing the geometric shape of your choice.

▶ To reverse the current color selections, try drawing with the right (or secondary) mouse button rather than the left. For example, to create a rectangle that's bordered by the current background color and filled with the foreground color, hold down the right mouse button as you drag the mouse.

▶ To quit the Paint program, choose Exit from the File menu or press Alt+F4.

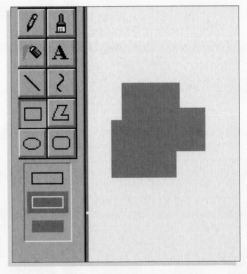

6 Now try using the new colors. Click the rectangle tool in the toolbox. In the options shown below the toolbox, select the middle setting for a bordered and filled rectangle. Move the mouse pointer into the drawing area and try creating two or three overlapping rectangles, holding down the left button as you drag the mouse. The current foreground color appears as the border for each rectangle you draw, and the background color is the fill.

2 To experiment with the width or shape setting, move the mouse pointer into the drawing area and draw a squiggle of any design. The brushstroke appears in the width you've selected.

3 Repeat steps 1 and 2 several times to try other widths and shape settings. When you've finished experimenting, press Ctrl+N (and then click No on the resulting dialog box) to clear the drawing area.

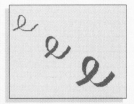

The foreground color

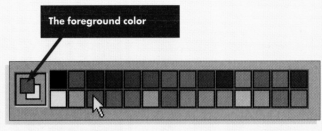

4 Move the mouse pointer into the palette. To select the foreground color, position the pointer over a color of your choice and click the *left* (or primary) mouse button. The new foreground color appears in the upper-left square in the box shown to the left of the palette.

The background color

5 To select the background color, move the pointer to a different color and click the *right* (or secondary) mouse button. The new background color appears in the lower-right square in the box shown to the left of the palette.

How to Use the Drawing Tools

As you've noticed by now, the freehand tools—including the pencil and the brush—are actually among the *most* demanding of Paint's drawing tools. They require you to move the mouse pointer precisely and deliberately to create an image on the screen. Other tools demand far less deftness and artistry for successful results. To use any tool, you position the mouse pointer over the tool's icon in the toolbox and click the left (or primary) mouse button. You can then select a width, shape, or other setting from the options shown below the toolbox. When you then move inside the drawing area, the mouse pointer appears in a shape that represents the tool you've selected.

TIP SHEET

▶ The "pick color" tool (shaped like an eyedropper) allows you to select foreground and background colors directly from the drawing area. Click the eyedropper tool and then move the mouse pointer into the drawing area, directly over an example of the color that you want to select. Then click the left mouse button to change the foreground color, or the right button to change the background color.

▶ The magnifier tool (located just to the right of the eyedropper tool) enlarges a portion of a picture and allows you to make detailed changes. Click the tool, and then select the portion of your drawing that you want to change. An enlarged view of the picture appears in the drawing area. You can now select another drawing tool to make changes in the enlargment.

▶ **1** To draw a straight line, select the line tool and move the mouse pointer to a starting position in the drawing area. Hold down the left mouse button to draw in the foreground color, or the right mouse button to draw in the background color, and drag the mouse through the length of the line you want to create. (Hold down the Shift key to draw a vertical, horizontal, or diagonal line.) Then release the mouse button.

8 To erase a portion of your drawing, select the eraser tool and then select an eraser width from the options shown below the toolbox. Hold down the left mouse button, and drag the mouse over the area you want to erase. The eraser tool replaces everything in its path with the background color.

7 To add text to your drawing, select the text tool. Drag the mouse through a rectangular area to create a text box. Optionally, select a font, point size, and styles from the text toolbar. (If the toolbar doesn't automatically appear on the screen, pull down the View menu and choose Text Toolbar.) Then begin typing the text from the keyboard. To start a new line, press Enter. Click elsewhere in the drawing area to complete the current text.

6 To fill an enclosed area with color, select the "fill with color" tool (shaped like a paint can) and move the mouse pointer to a position inside the area you want to fill. Click the left mouse button to fill with the current foreground color, or the right mouse button to fill with the background color.

2 To draw a curve, select the curve tool and use the mouse to draw a line across the area where you want the curve to appear. Then hold down the mouse button and drag in a direction perpendicular to the line; when the line forms the curve that you want, release the mouse button. Repeat this dragging action to produce a second curve in the line. When you release the mouse button again, the curve is complete.

3 To draw a rectangle, a rounded rectangle, a circle, or an oval, select the appropriate tool in the toolbox and then select a border or fill setting among the options shown below the toolbox. Use the left and right mouse buttons to select border and fill colors from the palette. Then drag the mouse in the drawing area to produce an outline of the shape that you want. Release the mouse button to complete the process. If you draw with the left (or primary) mouse button, the border appears in the foreground color and the fill is the background color. If you draw with the right (or secondary) button, the colors are reversed.

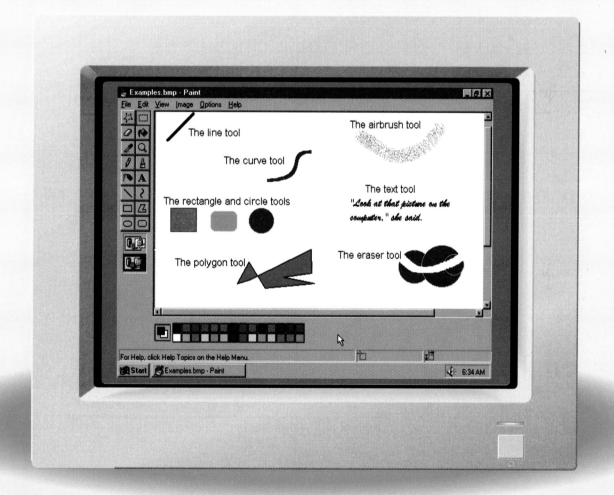

5 To create a spray paint effect, select the airbrush tool and then select a spray width in the box of options shown beneath the toolbox. Move the mouse pointer to a starting position in the drawing area. Hold down the mouse button and drag the mouse through the area you want to spray. Use the left button to spray in the foreground color, or the right to spray in the background color.

4 To draw a multisided figure, select the polygon tool and begin by drawing a line. Then reposition and click the mouse once to define each corner of the figure you want to create. To complete the shape, double-click the mouse at the final corner. The use of colors is the same as for rectangles and circles. (See step 3.)

How to Use a Cutout

A *cutout* is a portion of a drawing that you select for special actions. You can move a cutout, copy it, or *sweep* it to reproduce it many times along a path. A cutout is also the means of copying all or part of your drawing to the Clipboard; from there, the picture can be pasted to another application, such as a WordPad document. The two tools in the first row of the toolbox allow you to define either a freehand or rectangular cutout. In either case, the cutout is marked by dotted lines around the perimeter of the selection. Once you've defined a cutout, you use the mouse to move, copy, or sweep the picture it contains.

The freehand cutout tool

The rectangular cutout tool

▶ **1** Create a sample drawing to use in experiments with the cutout tools. Then click one of the two tools in the top row of the toolbox.

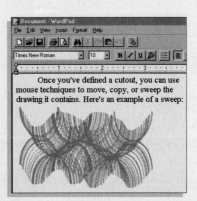

6 To copy a selection from the Paint program to another application, define a cutout and press Ctrl+C. Then start the other application and press Ctrl+V to paste the selection from the Clipboard.

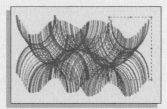

5 To sweep a drawing, first define a cutout. Then hold down the Shift key while you drag the selection through a sweep path. Release the mouse button and click elsewhere in the drawing area to deselect the cutout.

TIP SHEET

▶ **When you select a cutout tool, the two options that appear beneath the toolbox represent** *opaque* **and** *transparent* **cutout settings. These settings determine what happens when you move a cutout over the top of an existing drawing. Under the opaque setting, the cutout completely covers the equivalent area of the existing drawing. Under the transparent setting, the existing drawing appears as the background of the cutout.**

▶ **The Image menu provides special commands for changing the picture in a defined cutout. You can flip, rotate, stretch, and tilt the cutout, and you can invert its colors. Another way to select these options is to click inside a cutout with the right (or secondary) mouse button. The resulting pop-up menu shows a variety of commands related to the cutout and its contents.**

• **To change the dimensions of a cutout, position the mouse pointer over one of the** *size handles* **displayed along the dotted border and drag the mouse to increase or decrease the size of the picture contained in the cutout.**

2 Move the mouse pointer to a starting position in the drawing area. Hold down the left (or primary) mouse button and drag around the area you want to define as a cutout. When you release the mouse button, a border of dotted lines marks the cutout.

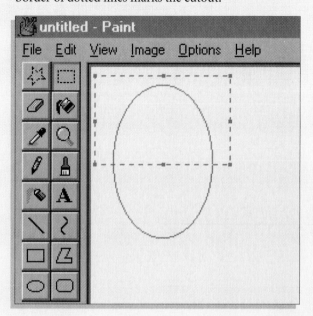

3 To move the cutout, position the mouse pointer inside the selected area, hold down the left mouse button, and drag the cutout to its new position. (The mouse pointer appears as a cross with four arrowheads.) When you're done with the cutout, move the mouse pointer elsewhere in the drawing area and click the left mouse button to deselect the drawing.

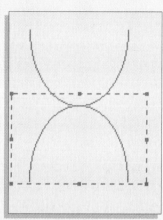

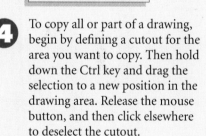

4 To copy all or part of a drawing, begin by defining a cutout for the area you want to copy. Then hold down the Ctrl key and drag the selection to a new position in the drawing area. Release the mouse button, and then click elsewhere to deselect the cutout.

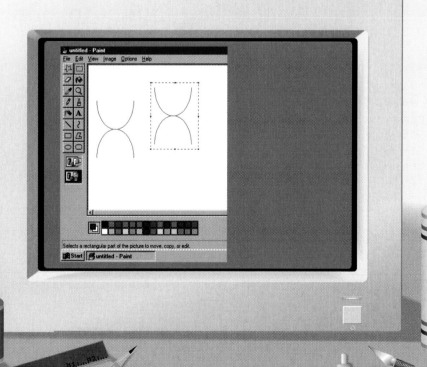

TRY IT!

I s there a "serious" business use for an amusing program like Paint? Here's an opportunity to find out. The owner of Hats 'n Ties, a specialty retail chain with several downtown locations, has asked you to come up with some ideas for her new logo and letterhead design. She wants a simple, snappy, whimsical logo that will instantly identify her business and fit in a variety of promotional materials. You've decided to use Paint to develop some initial designs.

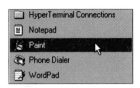

Click the Start button and choose Programs. Choose Accessories from the Programs menu, and then choose Paint from the Accessories menu. Click the Maximize button at the upper-right corner of the Paint window.

2

Using the right (or secondary) mouse button, click the light gray color selection in the palette (the second color in the lower row). Then click the oval tool in the toolbox and click the borderless rectangle below the toolbox.

3

Move the pointer into the drawing area. Hold down the left (or primary) mouse button and drag the mouse to draw an oval. Release the button. This light gray shape will become the face in the logo design.

4

Use the right mouse button to click dark gray in the palette, and draw a small filled circle beneath the gray oval. (Hold down the Shift key while you draw to form a circle.) This will be the knot of a tie.

5

Use the right mouse button to click the red color selection in the palette, and then draw another oval next to the first one.

6

Click the rectangle tool in the toolbox, and select the borderless rectangle below the toolbox.

7

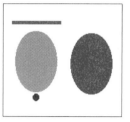

Move the pointer into the drawing area, and draw a thin red rectangle to serve as the rim of the hat.

8

Click the rectangular selection tool in the toolbox, and then use the right mouse button to click the white color selection in the palette.

9

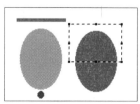

Move the pointer into the drawing area and define a cutout around the upper half of the red oval.

Continue to next page ▶

TRY IT!

Continue
below

10

Move the
mouse
pointer into
the cutout,
and drag the
shape to the
top of the red
rectangle. Together, the rectangle and
the half-circle form a hat.

11

Click the
eraser tool in
the toolbox
and use it to
erase the bot-
tom half of
the red oval.

12

Click the rec-
tangular se-
lection tool
again and de-
fine a cutout
around the entire hat. Then drag the
hat down into position on the head.

13

Define a
cutout
around the
entire draw-
ing. Hold
down the Ctrl key and drag the cutout
to the right to create a copy of the
drawing.

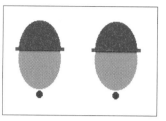

14

Select the
polygon tool
in the tool-
box and the unbordered solid shape in the option box beneath the toolbox. Then use the
right mouse button to click the dark gray color
selection in the palette. Draw two multisided
shapes that will serve as the long tie and the
bow tie.

15

Click the rec-
tangular selec-
tion tool and
use the right
mouse button
to select white
as the background color in the palette. Use
cutouts to drag both ties into place. Both versions of the logo are now complete.

16

Click the text
tool in the
toolbox.

Create a text box by dragging the mouse through a rectangular area in a blank space on the canvas. If the text toolbar doesn't automatically appear on the desktop, pull down the View menu and choose Text Toolbar.

In the Size box of the text toolbar, choose 14 as the point size for the current text. Then click the Bold button.

Type **Hats 'n Ties** into the text box you've created.

Drag the mouse to create a new text box just beneath the first line of text. In the text toolbar, select 12 as the point size, and click the Bold button to deactivate the boldface style. Then type the two lines of the address and the telephone number.

Hats 'n Ties
456 Allen Place
San Francisco, CA 94111

(415) 555-9876

Use cutouts to create a copy of the address and rearrange the logos and addresses in the drawing area.

Define a cutout around one version of the logo and address, and press Ctrl+C to copy the cutout to the Clipboard.

Start the WordPad application and press Ctrl+V to copy the logo and address to the top of the open document. Then print a copy of the document.

Go back to the Paint program, and repeat steps 22 and 23 to copy, paste, and print the second logo.

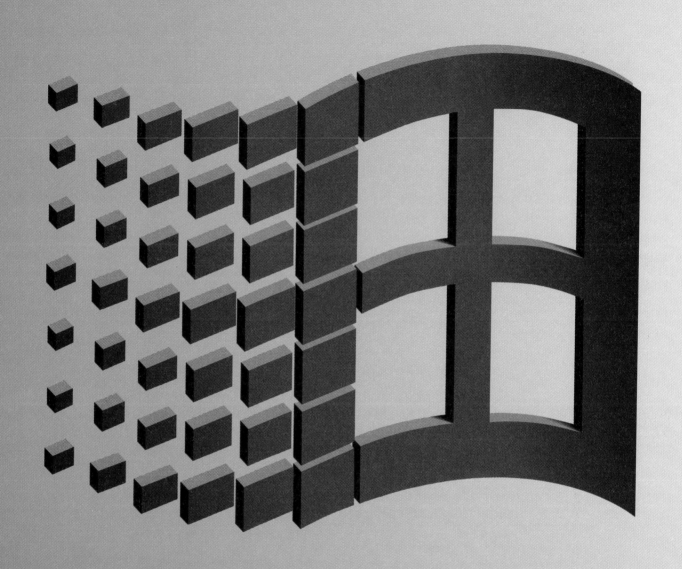

CHAPTER 14

More Word Processing Techniques

In this chapter and the next you'll revisit the WordPad application and expand your understanding of its features and capabilities. WordPad is a simple but practical word processing program. While it lacks many of the advanced tools available in more sophisticated programs, WordPad takes only a short time to learn and works reliably for long or short documents.

You've mastered the basics of WordPad already. Now turn your attention to a few of the fancier tricks, techniques, and shortcuts. In the upcoming pages you'll learn several new ways to work with text and to insert special characters into a document. You'll also examine the search and replace operations and a variety of settings that change the way the WordPad operates.

WordPad is an ideal environment for combining information from other applications into a single document. In Chapter 15, you'll learn how to use the techniques of *object linking and embedding* (OLE) to bring together information from a variety of sources.

How to Use Text Shortcuts

In Chapter 7 you learned the standard WordPad techniques for selecting text and changing the appearance of a document through a choice of fonts, styles, and point sizes. You've also seen how to use the Clipboard to move text from one place to another by the cut-and-paste method. Conveniently, WordPad offers a variety of shortcut techniques for all of these operations. Using your mouse, you can quickly select a line of text, move it to a new location in your document, and change its format.

The mouse pointer

▶ **①** To select a line of text, move the mouse pointer to the far left side of the WordPad window. The pointer takes the shape of a white arrow pointing diagonally up and to the right. Move the pointer vertically to the line that you want to select, and click the left (or primary) mouse button once. In response, WordPad selects the entire line of text.

TIP SHEET

▶ **There are several other ways to select a block of text in a WordPad document. Look back at "How to Apply Styles, Fonts, and Colors" in Chapter 7 for details.**

▶ **Shortcut menus are available throughout Windows 95 for changing the properties of objects on the desktop. To view a shortcut menu, you simply click an object with the right (or secondary) mouse button.**

▶ **Windows allows you to reverse the roles of the left and right mouse buttons, so that the right button works for primary operations like selecting text and the left button works for secondary operations like viewing shortcut menus. You may want to make this change if you're left-handed or if the reversal simply seems more comfortable to you. See "How to Change the Mouse Settings" in Chapter 4 for details.**

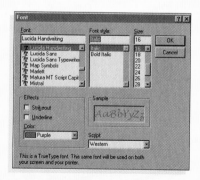

⑤ Choose the Font command from the shortcut menu. In the resulting font dialog box, select any new combination of options, including the font, style, size, and color. Click OK to confirm the changes.

2 To move a line of text to a new position in the document, begin by selecting the target text. Then position the mouse pointer over your selection. The pointer takes the shape of a white arrow, pointing diagonally up and to the left. Hold down the left (or primary) mouse button and drag the mouse pointer to the new position. The pointer becomes a solid vertical bar.

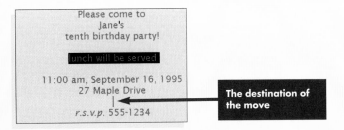

The destination of the move

Please come to
Jane's
tenth birthday party!

11:00 am, September 16, 1995
27 Maple Drive

lunch will be served

r.s.v.p. 555-1234

3 Release the mouse button to complete the move. WordPad moves the text to the position you've selected.

4 To change the appearance of a block of text, begin by selecting the text. Then position the mouse pointer over your selection and click the right (or secondary) mouse button. A shortcut menu of available operations appears on the screen. These include Cut, Copy, and Paste commands, along with a variety of formatting commands.

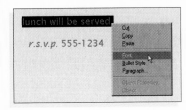

How to Search and Replace

As you compose a long document in WordPad, you may sometimes need a quick way to find a particular passage in your work. Rather than scroll through many pages of text, you can use the Find command to search instantly for the text you want to locate. Likewise, WordPad has a useful tool for making specific changes throughout your document. When you want to replace all instances of a word or phrase to something new, you can use the Replace command. Both Find and Replace are located in the Edit menu.

▶ **The "Match whole word only" option can be very important in search-and-replace operations. For example, if you're replacing *I* with *You* (as in the example shown on these pages), you would check this option to avoid changing the letter *i* in words like *lives*, *write*, *lists*, and *within*.**

▶ **After you complete a search-and-replace operation, you may have to go through your document and adjust capitalization in some instances of the replaced text. For example, "You" should be capitalized at the beginning of a sentence, but not within a sentence.**

▶ **You can click the Undo button on the toolbar (or choose Undo from the Edit menu) to undo the most recent replacement made in the text. But if you've clicked the Replace All button to carry out a change throughout your document, Undo does *not* restore the entire document to its original text; it only restores the final change.**

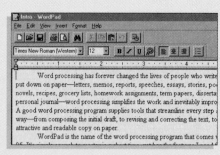

▶ **1** Choose WordPad from the Accessories list in the Start menu. When the WordPad window appears on the desktop, click the Open button on the toolbar, and open the document you want to examine or modify.

7 Alternatively, if you're sure you want to replace all instances of the text in a single operation, click the Replace All button.

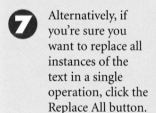

6 To replace instances of the target text one at a time, click the Find Next button to highlight the next instance of the text and then click Replace if you're sure you want to carry out the replacement. Repeat this step to search for and replace instances of the text throughout your document.

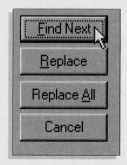

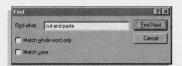

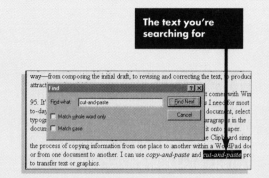

The text you're searching for

2 To search for a word or phrase in your document, pull down the Edit menu and choose Find, or click the Find button on the toolbar. In the Find dialog box, enter the text that you want to search for. As appropriate, check "Match whole word only" to avoid searching for text embedded within a word; check "Match case" to search for the text in the exact uppercase/lowercase combinations you've entered into the Find what box.

3 Click the Find Next button to search for the text. WordPad highlights the text you've specified. Click Cancel to close the Find dialog box.

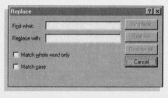

4 To replace all instances of a particular word or phrase, press Ctrl+Home to move to the top of the document, and choose the Replace command from the Edit menu. The Replace dialog box appears on the screen.

5 In the Find what box, enter the text you want to change. Then in the Replace with box enter the replacement text. Be careful to check "Match whole word only" if you want to avoid changing text embedded within words, and "Match case" if you want to replace only the exact text you've entered into the Find what box.

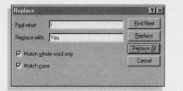

How to Use the Character Map

The Character Map is a simple Windows application that gives you convenient access to a variety of special symbols and characters, including a selection of whimsical line drawings known as *wingdings*. You can use the Character Map to choose any combination of these items and copy them to the Clipboard. Then you can insert the characters into a WordPad document.

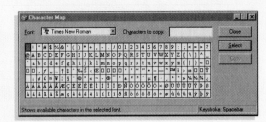

1 Choose Character Map from the Accessories list in the Start menu. The Character Map window appears on the desktop.

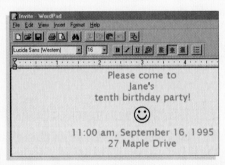

6 Click the Paste button on the toolbar (or press Ctrl+V from the keyboard) to insert the special character. Optionally, select the character and choose a new point size from the Font Size list; this step gives you the opportunity to increase the size of the character you've inserted.

5 Start WordPad and open the document in which you want to insert the special character you've chosen. Move the insertion point to the target position in the document.

TIP SHEET

▶ In addition to wingdings, the Character Map fonts include a variety of useful items, including mathematical symbols and other technical characters.

▶ You can also use the Character Map to produce typographical effects that are difficult to carry out from the keyboard. For example, you can insert curled quotation marks into a document.

▶ When you select a character in the Character Map, a notation at the lower-right corner of the application window shows you the keyboard shortcut for duplicating the character. You can use this shortcut as an alternative technique for inserting a symbol. For example, to insert a curled single quotation mark, hold down the Alt key and press 0146 at the keyboard's number pad.

2 Pull down the Font list and select the name of the font from which you want to choose a character. For example, to see a selection of small pictorial symbols, choose the Wingdings font. The grid beneath the font list shows the entire character set for the font you've selected.

Please come to
Jane's
tenth birthday party!
☺
11:00 am, September 16, 1995
27 Maple Drive

lunch will be served

r.s.v.p. ☎ 555-1234

The current character

A selected character

4 When you've found the character you want to use, click the Select button; the character appears in the box labeled "Characters to copy." Click the Copy button to copy the selection to the Clipboard. You can now minimize or close the Character Map window.

3 Use the arrow keys on the keyboard to select an individual character in the grid. The program enlarges the current character so you can see its details more clearly.

How to Change the WordPad Settings

There are several ways to modify the way WordPad operates. Probably the most important settings are found in the Page Setup dialog box. This command allows you to select a paper or envelope format for your document and to control other printing options. Additional settings are available in the Options dialog box, which appears when you choose the Options command from the View menu. This command offers word wrap modes, a variety of measurement units, and an important option that affects the use of the mouse to select text in a document.

An illustration of the print format

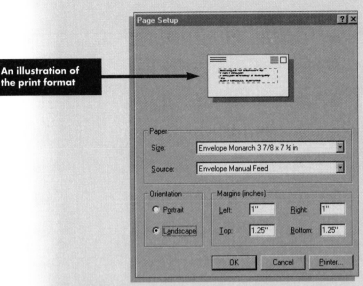

1 To change the printing format, pull down the File command and choose Page Setup. In the Page Setup dialog box, choose a paper or envelope format from the Size list and a manual or automatic paper feed option from the Source list. You can also choose between the Portrait and Landscape printing orientations, and you can adjust the four numeric margin settings. As you select among these options, an illustration at the top of the dialog box shows you what your printed document will look like.

TIP SHEET

▶ When you choose the New command from the File menu (or click the New button on the toolbar), WordPad displays a list of three file formats for you to choose from: Word 6, Rich Text, or Text. As you can see in step 2, these same formats appear on three of the tabs in the Options dialog box. The default file format is Word 6, which allows you to create a file that can also be modified in the Microsoft Word application. A Rich Text document (RTF) can include fonts and formatting, and can be modified in most major word processing programs. The Text format does not permit formatting options.

▶ To select options for the printer attached to your computer, choose the Print command from the File menu and click the Properties button on the resulting dialog box. In the Properties dialog box you can select a resolution for printing graphics, and modify other options that apply specifically to your printer.

2 For other settings, pull down the View menu and choose Options. The Options dialog box contains tabs for the various file formats you can produce from WordPad. Under each format you can choose a distinct word wrap option, specifying how WordPad will control the width of your text. You can also select the toolbars you want WordPad to display for a given file type.

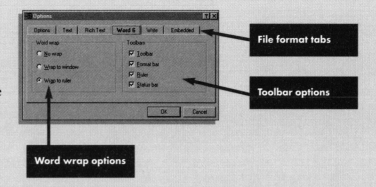

File format tabs

Toolbar options

Word wrap options

9000 Brush Street
San Francisco, CA 94109

Ms. Angie Giles
999 Fifth Place
San Francisco,
California 94123

The Options tab

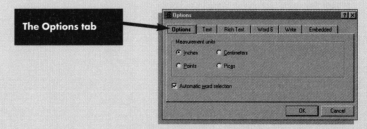

3 To change the units of measurement used throughout WordPad, click the Options tab and select among the four units: Inches, Centimeters, Points, or Picas. When you click OK to confirm, the ruler displays the new unit you've selected.

☑ Automatic word selection

4 Use the check box labeled "Automatic word selection" to change the way the mouse works for selecting text in WordPad. When the option is checked, WordPad selects an entire word at a time as you drag the mouse pointer across a line of text. When the option is unchecked, text selection advances by one character at a time.

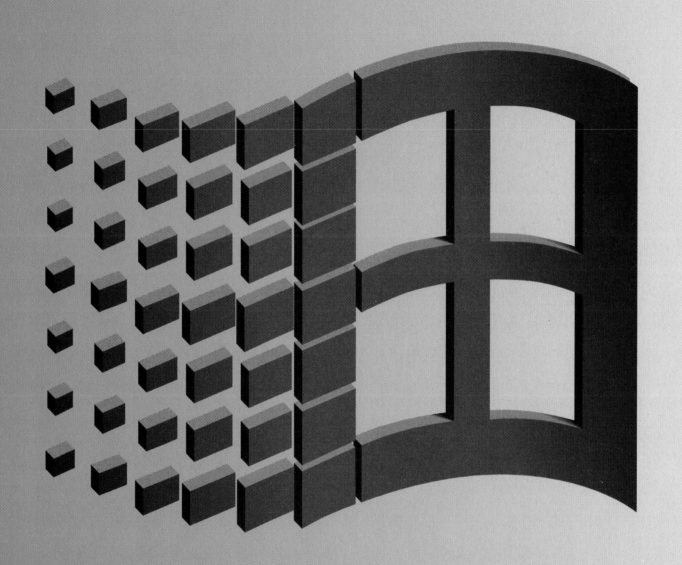

CHAPTER 15

Object Linking and Embedding

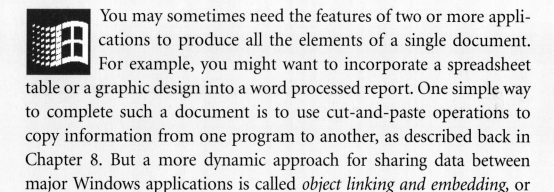You may sometimes need the features of two or more applications to produce all the elements of a single document. For example, you might want to incorporate a spreadsheet table or a graphic design into a word processed report. One simple way to complete such a document is to use cut-and-paste operations to copy information from one program to another, as described back in Chapter 8. But a more dynamic approach for sharing data between major Windows applications is called *object linking and embedding,* or OLE.

Using OLE techniques you can edit and update all the parts of a document you're developing, even if the information originates from different programs. Suppose you're using WordPad to prepare an expense report for a recent business trip. A central part of your document is a short table of expense data that you've compiled in a spreadsheet program. Halfway through your work you notice that you've made a mistake in one of the numbers in the expense table. Thanks to OLE, you can revise the spreadsheet table quickly and easily, without leaving your work in WordPad.

OLE offers two different techniques for data exchange. An *embedded* object provides all the features of a source application, but is independent of any existing file on disk. By contrast, a *linked* object is inserted in your current document and retains its connections to an original file on disk. If you make changes in the linked information, Windows automatically transfers those changes to the source file. You'll see examples of both these approaches in this chapter.

How to Insert Objects in WordPad

As you develop a document in WordPad, you can easily insert information from other applications. If the insertion exists only as part of your WordPad document, not as a separate file on disk, it is known as an *embedded object*. A typical example is a worksheet table incorporated into the text of a business document. Whatever application you use to create the table—Microsoft Excel, Lotus 1-2-3, or some other spreadsheet—you'll have all the program's features at your disposal whenever you activate the embedded object.

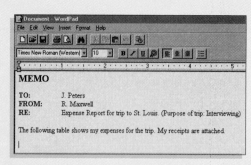

▶ **1** Start WordPad from the Accessories list in the Start menu. When the application window appears on the desktop, begin entering the text of your document.

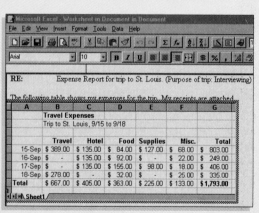

5 As you complete the object, you can use all the features of the application you've selected. For example, if the object is a spreadsheet, you can enter labels, values, and formulas, and you can format the result in any variety of ways. When you finish your work, click the mouse inside the text of the word processed document to deselect the object. As shown in the central graphic on these pages, the object appears as part of the document. You can now save your document to disk and print it if you wish.

2 When you reach the point where you want to insert an object, pull down WordPad's Insert menu and choose the New Object command. The Insert Object dialog box appears on the screen.

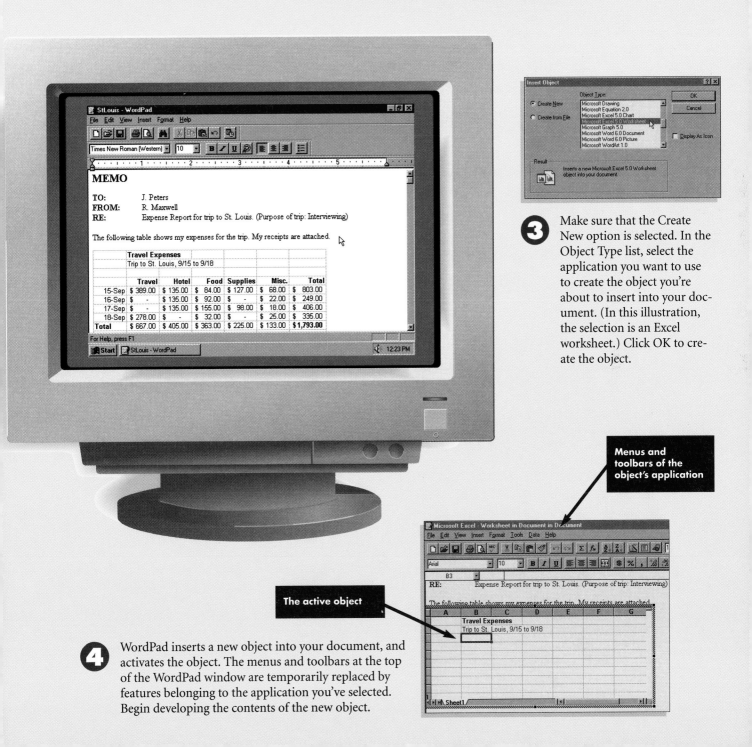

3 Make sure that the Create New option is selected. In the Object Type list, select the application you want to use to create the object you're about to insert into your document. (In this illustration, the selection is an Excel worksheet.) Click OK to create the object.

Menus and toolbars of the object's application

The active object

4 WordPad inserts a new object into your document, and activates the object. The menus and toolbars at the top of the WordPad window are temporarily replaced by features belonging to the application you've selected. Begin developing the contents of the new object.

How to Work with Embedded Objects

As you've seen, an embedded object appears as part of a document but is not linked to any other file on disk. When you activate an embedded object, you can edit its contents, using the tools and techniques available in the source application. The object can be activated directly in the host application window, or in a separate window that contains the source program.

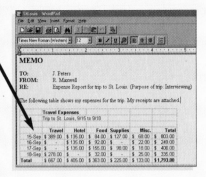

An embedded object

1 Open or create a document that contains an embedded object. (For details, see "How to Insert Objects in WordPad," on the previous two pages.)

TIP SHEET

▶ You can insert an existing file into a WordPad document as an embedded object. Choose the New Object command from the Insert menu. In the Insert Object dialog box, click the Create from File option. Then enter the path name of the target file into the File text box. Leaving the Link option unchecked, click OK to insert the object. Because this object is not linked to its source file, you can edit the information without affecting the original file. (For more information about the Create from File option, turn the page.)

▶ Another way to embed a worksheet into a WordPad document is to select the worksheet information in its own application window, and press Ctrl+C to copy the selection to the Clipboard. Then switch to WordPad and choose Paste Special from the Edit menu. On the Paste Special dialog box, click OK to create the embedded object.

5 To experiment further, try clicking the embedded object with the right (or secondary) mouse button. In the resulting shortcut menu, select the last command ("Worksheet Object" in this example). The resulting cascade menu contains two options for activating the object: You can choose Edit to activate the embedded object within the host application, as shown in step 2, above. Alternatively, choose Open to activate the embedded object within a separate application window. Either way, all the features of the source application are available for working with the object.

2 Position the mouse pointer over the embedded object and double-click the left (or primary) mouse button. This step activates the object so that you can edit its contents. At the top of the host application window, you'll see the menus and toolbars belonging to the program in which you created the object.

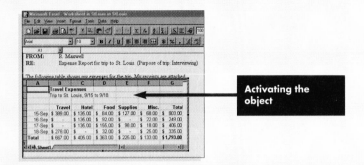

Activating the object

Embedding

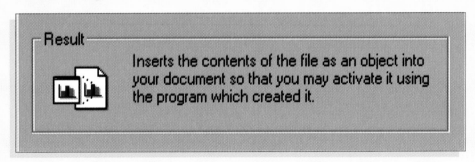

A change in the object's contents

3 Make any changes in the contents of the embedded object. The object behaves just as it would in its source application. (In this illustration, changing a value in the worksheet table results in an instant recalculation of all the formulas that depend on the value.)

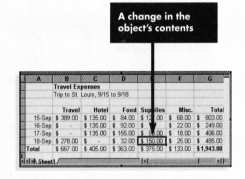

4 To deactivate the object, click outside its borders in the host document. You can now save your work to disk and print the document if you wish. The embedded object will be printed as part of the document.

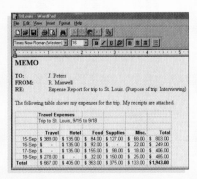

How to Work with Linked Objects

A *linked object* adds the contents of an existing file to the document you're currently producing. When you activate the object and make changes in its contents, Windows automatically updates the source file to reflect the revisions. Conversely, if you edit the original file, the changes are transferred to the linked object in the document you're developing.

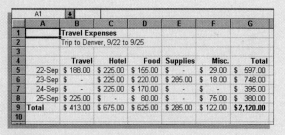

 1 Develop the document that you plan to use as the source of a linked object. In this illustration, the document is a worksheet table created in Microsoft Excel. Save the document to disk, and then close the application if you wish.

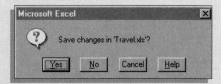

6 In response to the "Save changes" prompt, click the Yes button. Your revisions are transferred forward to the linked object in your document.

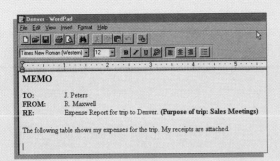

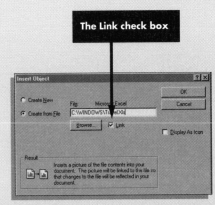

The Link check box

2 Create a WordPad document in which you want to insert the linked object. Move the flashing cursor to the position where you want to insert the object.

3 Pull down the Insert menu and choose the New Object command. In the resulting dialog box, click the Create from File option. In the File box, enter the full path name of the file you want to insert. Finally, select the Link option, placing a check mark in the corresponding box, and click OK.

Linking

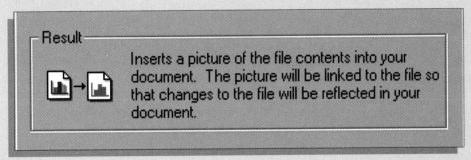

┌─Result─────────────────────────────────
Inserts a picture of the file contents into your document. The picture will be linked to the file so that changes to the file will be reflected in your document.

A linked object

4 The new object appears in your document at the current cursor position. Double-click the object to activate it. A separate application window appears on the desktop to display the contents of the linked object.

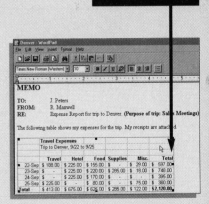

5 Make any changes in the contents of the object. Then pull down the File menu and choose Exit to return to your original document.

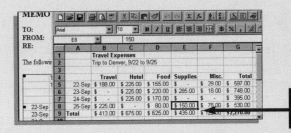

A change in the object's contents

TRY IT!

In this exercise you'll practice the OLE techniques that you learned about in Chapter 15. Specifically, you'll create a WordPad document and then you'll insert a worksheet as a linked object. The owner of Hats 'n Ties (the specialty retail chain you've worked with elsewhere in this book) has used Microsoft Excel to compile a table of fourth-quarter sales totals from all five of her downtown stores. She wants to include this information in a memo that she'll distribute to her staff. As you go through the steps of creating this document, you can substitute your own sales data if you want. If you don't have Excel, you can use any other spreadsheet program that's installed on your computer.

Start Microsoft Excel, or any other spreadsheet program that's installed on your computer.

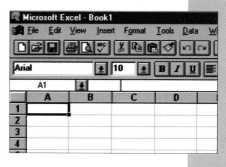

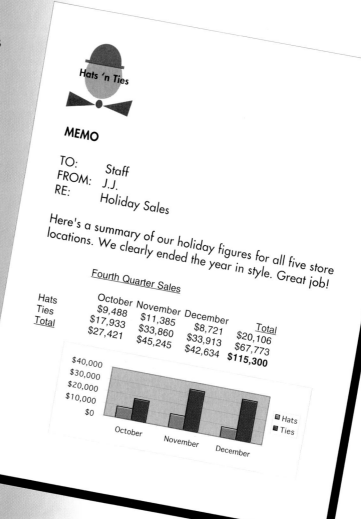

Hats 'n Ties

MEMO

TO: Staff
FROM: J.J.
RE: Holiday Sales

Here's a summary of our holiday figures for all five store locations. We clearly ended the year in style. Great job!

Fourth Quarter Sales

	October	November	December	Total
Hats	$9,488	$11,385	$8,721	$20,106
Ties	$17,933	$33,860	$33,913	$67,773
Total	$27,421	$45,245	$42,634	**$115,300**

2

Enter a table of sales figures, including a row and column of calculated totals. (In Excel you can produce a range of totals simply by selecting the range and clicking the AutoSum button on the toolbar.)

3

Create a graph from your sales data. (Use the ChartWizard in Excel to guide you through the steps of creating the graph.)

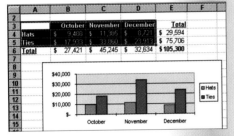

4

Pull down the File menu and choose Save As. Save your worksheet file in the Windows folder as 4QSales. Then close the spreadsheet program.

5

Start WordPad from the Accessories list in the Start menu.

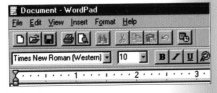

6

Optionally, use a simple copy-and-paste operation from the Paint program to insert a logo at the top of your document. (The design shown here is a variation of the logo you created in the Try It exercise following Chapter 13.)

7

Beneath the logo, type the text of your memo.

8

Move the cursor to the bottom of your document. Then pull down the Insert menu and choose New Object.

9

The Insert Object dialog box appears on the screen. Click the Create from File option.

Continue to next page ▶

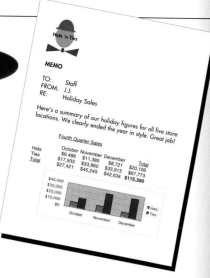

TRY IT!

Continue below

10

Click the Browse button.

11

Use the Browse window to locate the sales worksheet file in the Windows folder. When you select the file's name, WordPad copies the name to the File name box.

12

Click the Insert button to close the Browse window and return to the Insert Object dialog box. The complete path name of the target file now appears in the File box.

13

Click the Link option. A check appears in the corresponding box.

14

Click OK to insert the sales worksheet as a linked object in your WordPad file.

15

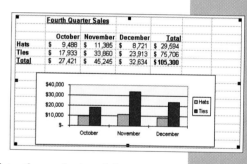

Take a close look at the worksheet object. Suppose you now find an error in your original sales data; the total sales of ties in December should appear as $33,913.

16

Double-click the worksheet object to activate it for editing. The worksheet appears inside its own application window.

17

Enter **$33,913** as the corrected sales figure for ties in December. When you complete the correction, Excel automatically re-calculates the totals and redraws the chart.

18

Pull down the File menu and choose the Exit command.

19

Excel asks you if you want to save the changes you've made to the original file. Click the Yes button.

20

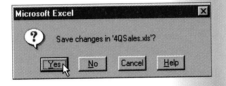

Back in the WordPad window, click the Save button on the toolbar and save your document as Sales.Doc.

21

Click the Print Preview button on the WordPad toolbar.

22

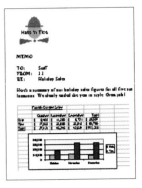

In the Preview window, examine your document and make sure it's formatted the way you want it. Then click the Print button to print a copy of your memo. Click OK on the Print dialog box.

23

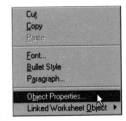

To explore further, click the work-sheet object with the right (or secondary) mouse button and choose Object Properties from the resulting shortcut menu.

24

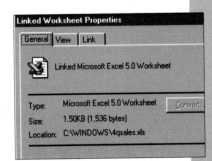

The Linked Worksheet Properties window gives you information about the linked object and allows you to make changes in the characteristics of the link. Click each of the tabs in turn to see what options are available. Then click OK to close the box.

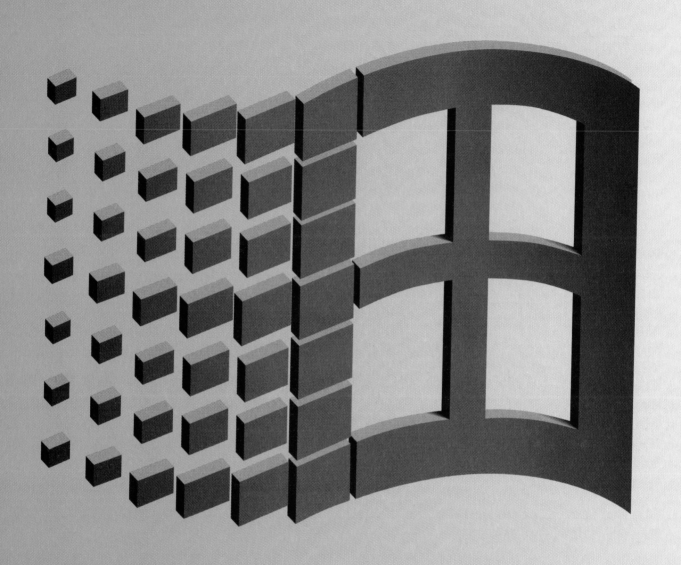

CHAPTER 16

Installing New Hardware and Software

As your computing needs change over time, you may find yourself acquiring new hardware and software for your PC. Thanks to Windows 95, expanding your system has never been easier. No matter what you decide to add—a new printer, a CD-ROM drive, the latest spreadsheet program, or a video game for the kids—Windows ensures a simple and reliable installation process.

In this chapter you'll focus on two sets of tools, both located in the Control Panel. The Hardware Wizard helps you complete the installation of the most common types of hardware you're likely to add to your computer. The Add/Remove Programs tool guides you through the steps of installing new applications or adding uninstalled components of Windows 95 to the desktop.

In the final pages of this chapter you'll learn to create a special *startup* disk, designed to help you recover gracefully from system failure if anything should ever go wrong with your installation of Windows.

How to Use the Hardware Wizard

When you add a new piece of hardware to your computer system—a printer, a modem, a new input device, a CD-ROM drive, or any other item—you'll want to make sure that Windows 95 recognizes the new device and uses it successfully. The Hardware Wizard will help you complete the installation process. If your new hardware package includes a "driver" program, keep the disk handy as you begin these steps.

1 Click the Start button and choose Settings. Then choose Control Panel from the Settings list.

Manufacturers   **Hardware models**

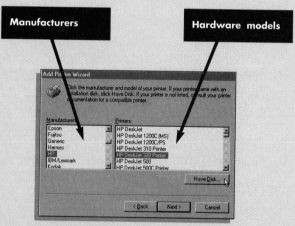

5 The next window contains a list of manufacturers and a corresponding list of hardware models. Select the manufacturer's name and then select the model from the list on the right. If you have a disk containing the driver for the hardware, click the Have Disk button at this point. If not, click Next and be prepared to use your original Windows disk (or disks) to complete the installation. Either way, the Wizard will instruct you to insert the appropriate disk and then will guide you through any remaining steps required for the particular item you're installing.

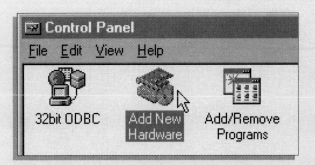

2 When the Control Panel window appears on the desktop, double-click the icon labeled "Add New Hardware."

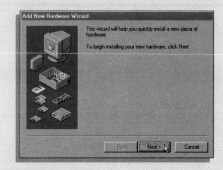

3 The first window of the Add New Hardware Wizard appears on the screen. Click the Next button to begin installing your new hardware.

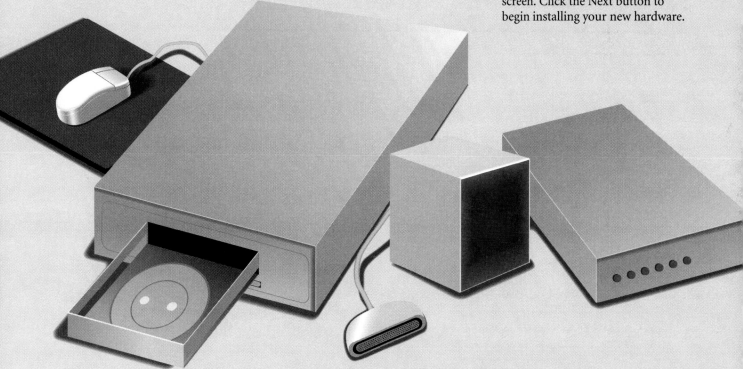

4 The next window gives you the option of letting Windows search for your new hardware. If you prefer to identify the hardware yourself, select No and click Next. A list of hardware categories appears in the next window. Scroll through the list and select the type of hardware you want to install. Then click Next to continue.

How to Add Windows Components

Windows 95 has many components and applications, some of which may *not* be included automatically in your system's default installation. To avoid taking up space on your hard disk with options you don't plan to use, Windows lets you decide which elements to install. For example, several of the features described in this book—including the Briefcase, the game programs, the Microsoft Network software, the accessibility aids, and others— may be missing initially from your Start menu or your desktop. If you want to use these components, you'll have to install them directly from the original Windows 95 disk or disks.

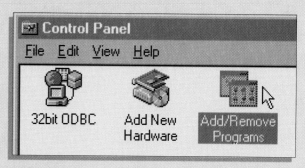

1 Click the Start menu, choose Settings, and click the Control Panel option. When the Control Panel window appears on the desktop, double-click the Add/Remove Programs icon.

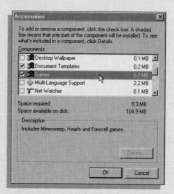

5 A new window shows the specific items available in the category you've chosen. Click each option that you want to install, placing a check mark in the corresponding box. Then click OK on the active window and OK again on the Add/Remove Programs window. Windows prompts you to insert the disk that's required for the new installation. (If you originally installed windows from CD-ROM, you should insert the disk at this time.)

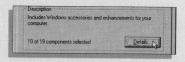

4 Notice that the Description box (below the Components list) provides a brief description of the category you've chosen. Click the Details button to continue your selection.

TIP SHEET

▶ After installing a new component, Windows updates the shortcuts to the new feature. In many cases, this may mean that a new entry will appear in the Applications list or in some other part of the Start menu. For other components—such as the Microsoft Network and the Briefcase—a new icon may appear directly on the desktop. (See the central graphic on these pages for an example of the Briefcase icon. Turn to Chapter 17 for information about using the Briefcase.)

▶ In the Components list, a gray check box indicates an incomplete installation in this category; some of the applications have been installed and others have not.

▶ Another way to open the Control Panel window is to double-click the My Computer icon and then double-click the Control Panel icon.

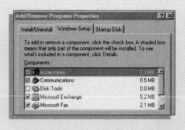

2 A window entitled "Add/Remove Programs Properties" appears. Three tabs are arranged along the top of the window. Click the Windows Setup tab.

3 The Components list shows you the major categories of applications and options available in Windows 95. Select the category of the item you want to install.

The Briefcase, Fax, and Games applications may all require separate installation steps.

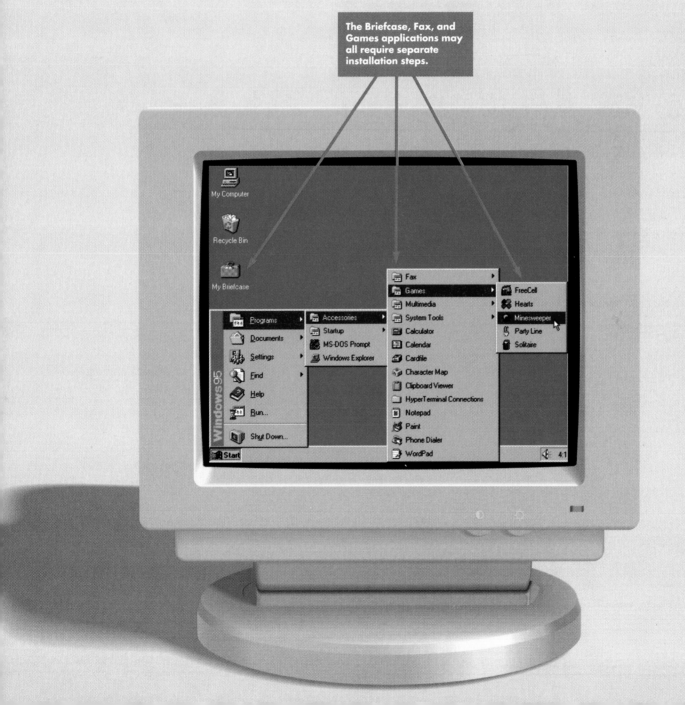

How to Install and Uninstall Other Software

When you buy a new software package for your computer, the first thing you generally need to do is run the installation program for the application. The Add/Remove Programs tool gives you a simple way to carry out this task. Furthermore, you can use the Add/Remove window to *un*install a program that you don't use any more. Windows applications often install files in several different directories on your hard disk, and sometimes share components with other software; for these reasons, removing a program can be difficult and even risky. The Remove tool now does the job safely and systematically.

TIP SHEET

▶ As a general rule, you should close any programs that are running on the desktop before you try installing a new application. Otherwise, conflicts can occur during the installation process.

▶ You can also use the Run window to install a new application. Insert the installation disk and then choose Run from the Start menu. In the Open box, enter the path and file name of the installation program, and click OK.

▶ Like Windows itself, many applications offer two or three different ways to complete an installation. The default installation generally includes a program's most commonly used features. If you later decide that you want more features, you can run the installation program again and choose the components you want to add. (See "How to Add Windows Components" on the previous page to review the steps for adding features to your Windows installation.)

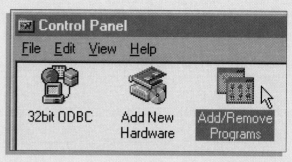

▶ **1** Click the Start button and choose Settings. Then choose Control Panel from the Settings list. In the Control Panel window, double-click the Add/Remove Programs icon.

 The following software can be automatically removed by Windows. To remove a program, select it from the list and click Remove.

5 To remove an application from your system, select a name from the list of removable programs in the lower half of the Install/Uninstall tab. Then click the Remove button.

4 Follow the instructions on the screen to complete the installation. For an installation from floppy disks, you'll be told when to remove the current disk and insert the next one.

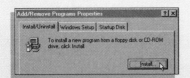

2 In the Add/Remove Programs Properties window, click the Install/Uninstall tab if necessary. Then click the Install button when you're ready to install your new software.

3 When you see the window entitled "Install Programs From Floppy Disk or CD-ROM," insert the disk for the new application. (If the application is delivered on a set of floppy disks, the first one is generally the installation disk.) Then click the Next button. Windows locates the disk and starts the installation program.

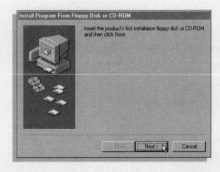

How to Create a Startup Disk

Windows 95 is a reliable operating system, but unpredictable problems sometimes occur, especially as you begin installing new software on your computer. As a safeguard, you should always have a *startup disk* that you can use to boot your computer in the event that something goes wrong with Windows. You may have created a startup disk when you originally installed Windows on your computer. If not—or if the disk is lost—you can use the Add/Remove tool to create a new one.

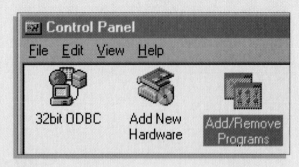

1 Click the Start menu, choose Settings, and then choose Control Panel. In the Control Panel window, double-click the Add/Remove Programs icon.

4 Click OK on the Insert Disk window when you're ready to begin creating the startup disk. When the process is complete, remove the floppy disk, label it appropriately, and put it in a safe place where you'll find it if you ever need it. (Also remove the Windows 95 disk and put it back in its box.)

TIP SHEET

▶ **In addition to the system software necessary for booting your computer, the startup disk contains tools designed to help you find and correct any problems that occur in Windows.**

▶ **If you've installed Windows on more than one computer, create a separate startup disk for each system, and label each disk appropriately.**

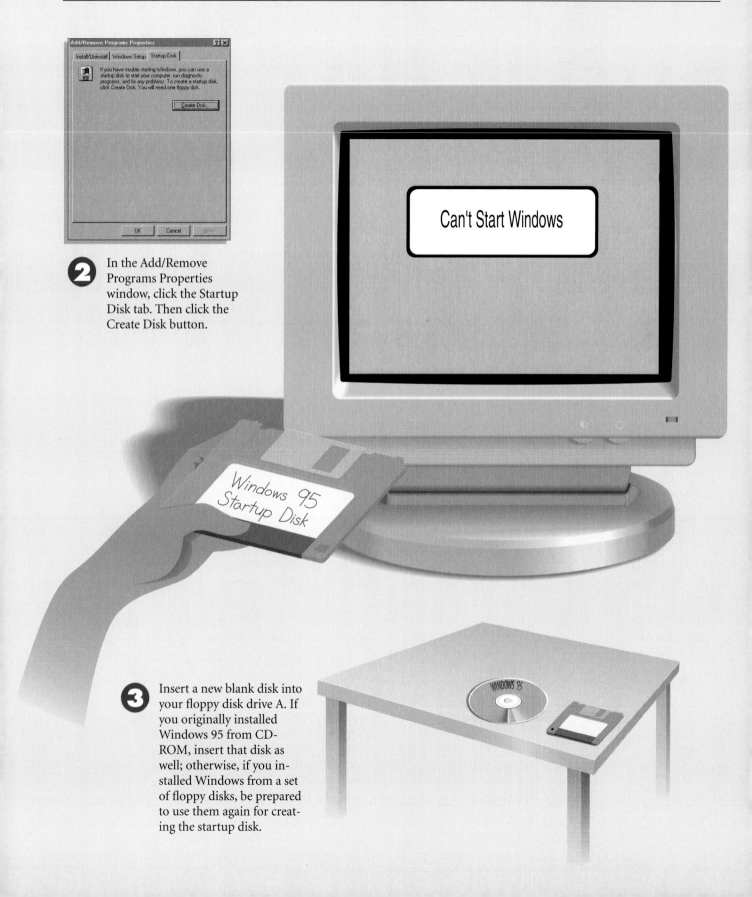

Can't Start Windows

2 In the Add/Remove Programs Properties window, click the Startup Disk tab. Then click the Create Disk button.

Windows 95 Startup Disk

3 Insert a new blank disk into your floppy disk drive A. If you originally installed Windows 95 from CD-ROM, insert that disk as well; otherwise, if you installed Windows from a set of floppy disks, be prepared to use them again for creating the startup disk.

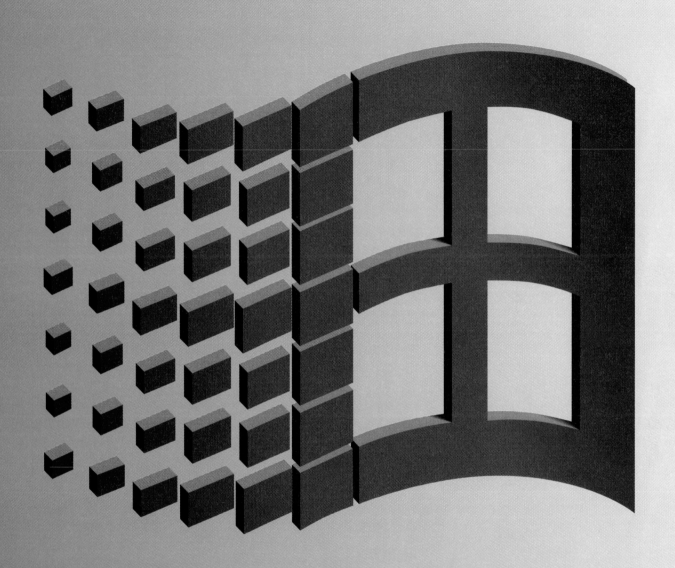

CHAPTER 17

Working with Briefcase

If you're a frequent business traveler, you probably have two computers—a desktop system at the office, and a laptop machine for computing on the road. This convenience poses a logistical dilemma: How do you coordinate your work on the two machines, always making sure that both systems contain the latest versions of all your important files? For example, suppose you make changes in a budget worksheet and half a dozen related data files on your laptop; what's the most *reliable* way to transfer these important revisions to the original files on your desktop computer?

Briefcase is a tool designed to solve this problem efficiently. Before you go on a trip, you can create a Briefcase on your main computer and store copies of all the files that you're planning to revise while you're gone. During your trip, you use your laptop machine to access these files directly from the Briefcase.

Back at the office, you open your Briefcase and choose the Update command to transfer the revised files to your desktop computer. The update takes place in one simple operation. After this step, you can be sure that both computers contain the same versions of your files and that all information is current.

You can create any number of Briefcase icons on your desktop or disks, but first you need to make sure that the Briefcase software is installed. If it's not available, turn to "How to Add Windows Components" in Chapter 16 for installation instructions.

How to Get Started with Briefcase

ABriefcase on a floppy disk is an ideal tool for managing data files when you travel. Inside the Briefcase you store copies of the files you'll need while you're gone. Then you take the floppy disk with you on your trip and use it for all your work on the target files.

1 Insert a blank disk into your floppy drive. Open the My Computer window and double-click the icon for the disk. A window representing the disk appears on the desktop.

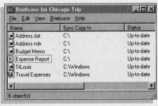

5 Now double-click the Briefcase icon to review the collection of files you've prepared. Notice that the Briefcase window lists the status of each file as "Up-to-date" at this point. Your Briefcase is now ready for your upcoming trip. Close the window and remove the floppy disk from your desktop machine. To see how to use this disk, turn the page.

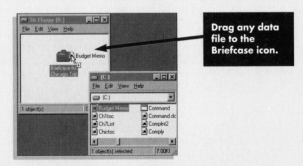

Drag any data file to the Briefcase icon.

4 Inside the My Computer window, double-click the hard-disk icon and then open any folder that contains a file you want to take on your trip. Drag the file icon to the Briefcase you've created on your floppy disk. When you do so, Windows copies the file to the Briefcase. Repeat this step for each of the files you want to place in your Briefcase.

TIP SHEET

▶ **In the Briefcase you can store files from any combination of folders on your hard disk. To ensure a reliable update, the Briefcase keeps track of each file's original location.**

▶ **If your floppy disk doesn't have the capacity for all the files you want to store in your briefcase, consider using the DriveSpace utility to compress the disk. This will approximately double the disk's capacity. See "How to Use DriveSpace" in Chapter 22 for details.**

▶ **Another way to share Briefcase files is to set up a direct cable connection between your two computers. The Direct Cable Connection software is an accessory you can install in your system from the original Windows 95 disk (or disks).**

2 Click inside the window with the right (or secondary) mouse button and choose New from the resulting menu. Then choose Briefcase from the New menu. A Briefcase icon appears in the disk window. (If you don't see Briefcase in the New menu, you need to install the Briefcase software on your system. See Chapter 16 for details.)

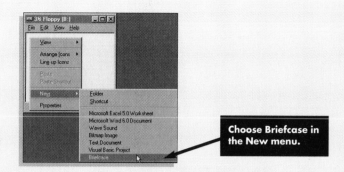

Choose Briefcase in the New menu.

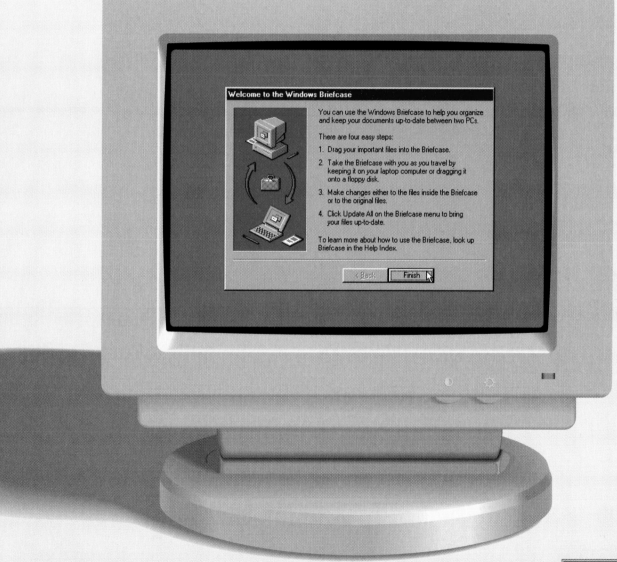

3 Click the Briefcase icon with the right (or secondary) mouse button and choose Rename from the shortcut menu. Then type a new name that identifies the use you're planning for the Briefcase. Press Enter to confirm the name change. At this point, you might want to try double-clicking the Briefcase icon; when you do so, a Welcome window appears on the desktop, as shown in the central graphic on these pages. Read the introduction it contains, and then close it by clicking Finish. For now, close the Briefcase window as well.

How to Work with Briefcase Files

While you're on the road—using your laptop computer as a portable system—you can work with any of the files you've stored in your Briefcase. The Briefcase keeps track of the files you modify. Then when you arrive back at the office, you can quickly update your work on your desktop computer.

▶ **①** During your trip, insert the floppy disk containing your Briefcase into your laptop computer. All the files you've placed in your Briefcase are now available for you to use and revise.

▶ **You can also update files individually from the Briefcase window. Using the right (or secondary) mouse button, click the name of a file that needs updating, and choose Update from the resulting shortcut menu. The Briefcase copies the revised file to its original location on your main computer.**

▶ **In the Update Briefcase window (step 5) you can change the action that will take place as a result of an update. Click any file icon with the right (or secondary) mouse button to view a menu of options. Choose the right-arrow icon to replace the file on your main computer with the file in the briefcase (the default action). Choose the left-arrow icon to replace the Briefcase file with the original file stored on your main computer. Choose the Skip option to take no action on the file you've selected. When you've chosen an action for each file that needs updating, click the Update button to carry out these actions.**

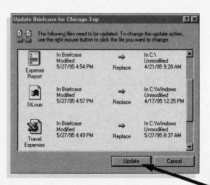

⑤ To update the original files, pull down the Briefcase menu and choose Update All. In the resulting window, click the Update button to complete the update procedure.

Click Update to replace the original files.

2 On your laptop, start an application in which you can work with one of your briefcase files. Choose the Open command from the application's File menu, and open your file directly from the Briefcase on your floppy disk.

Open a file from the Briefcase.

3 Revise the file in any way you wish. To save your revisions back to the Briefcase, simply click the application's Save button, or choose Save from the File menu. During your travels, you might repeat these steps many times to revise files in your Briefcase.

4 When you return to the office, insert the floppy disk into your desktop computer. From the My Computer window, open the window for the floppy drive and double-click the Briefcase icon to view its current contents. The files that you revised during your trip are now labeled "Needs updating."

These are the files you've revised.

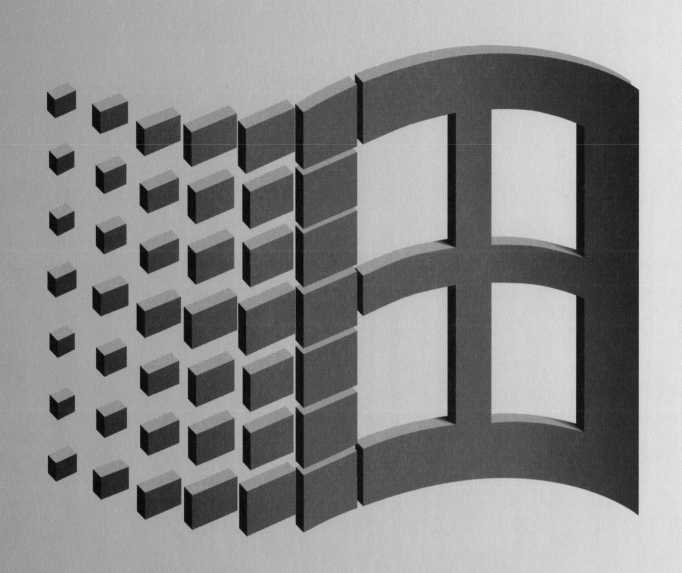

CHAPTER 18

Sending and Receiving Faxes

If your computer is equipped with a fax/modem, you can use tools in Windows 95 to send and receive fax transmissions and to organize the resulting messages on your computer. To find out whether the appropriate software has been installed on your system yet, look for the following items:

- The Inbox icon, located directly on the desktop. This icon represents an application called Microsoft Exchange, a central location for all kinds of message-handling in Windows 95.

- The Fax folder in the Start menu's Accessories list. This folder provides several options, including "Compose New Fax," which starts a simple step-by-step program known as the *Fax Wizard*.

If these programs are missing, you'll need to install them before you try to send or receive a fax. The first topic in this chapter ("How to Use the Fax Wizard") shows the selection you'll need to make in the Add/Remove Programs window to complete the installation. You can also turn back to Chapter 16 for complete information about adding Windows 95 components to your system.

In this chapter you'll learn two different ways to send a fax—using the Fax Wizard, or sending a document directly from an application. You'll also find out how to design your own cover pages and how to prepare your system for receiving a fax.

How to Use the Fax Wizard

The Fax Wizard guides you quickly and easily through the steps of preparing an outgoing fax transmission. You identify the recipient, supply the fax number, choose a cover page, and compose a message. When you've completed these steps, Windows creates the message and sends the fax.

1 If the Fax folder is not available in the Accessories list of your Start menu, double-click the Add/Remove Programs icon in the Control Panel, and install Microsoft Fax from your original Windows 95 disk. (See "How to Add Windows Components" in Chapter 16 for complete instructions.) Windows also installs Microsoft Exchange if it is not already available. When the installation is complete, a new icon named Inbox appears on your desktop and the Fax software is available from the Start menu. The first time you use the Fax Wizard, it asks you for information about your own fax location—name, fax number, and so on. This information appears on the cover page you choose for a fax transmission.

TIP SHEET

▶ **If you want to revise the information about your own fax location—that is, the information that Windows transfers automatically to the cover page you select—double-click the Inbox icon to open Microsoft Exchange. Then pull down the Tools menu, choose Microsoft Fax Tools, and choose Options from the resulting menu. In the resulting dialog box, click the User tab. Make any necessary changes in the information (name, fax number, company, address, phone numbers, and so on) and then click OK.**

▶ **For a complete set of help topics about Microsoft Fax, double-click the Inbox icon. In the Microsoft Exchange window, pull down the Help menu and choose Microsoft Fax Help Topics. You'll find information about the Fax Wizard, Microsoft Exchange, cover pages, and modem setup. There's also a Troubleshooting section you can use to solve hardware or software problems related to fax transmissions.**

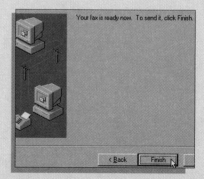

6 On the final window, click Finish to send the fax. The Fax Wizard prepares your complete transmission, dials the fax number, and sends the message along with the cover page you've selected. A window named Microsoft Fax Status appears on the desktop to report the progress of the transmission.

2 When you're ready to send a fax, make sure your modem is operating and your phone line is connected properly. Then click the Start menu and choose Accessories. From the list of programs, choose Fax and click Compose New Fax. The first window of the Fax Wizard appears on the desktop, giving you the opportunity to change the way calls are made from your modem. (See the central graphic on these pages.) Click Next to begin preparing a fax.

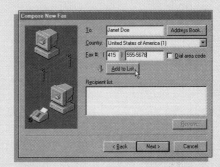

3 Enter the name and fax number of the person to whom you want to send a fax. Then click the Add to list button to copy this name to the Recipients list. Repeat this step if you want to send copies of the fax to more than one destination. Then click Next to continue.

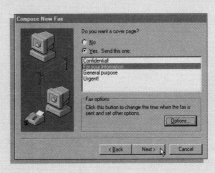

5 In the next window, type a brief description of the subject and then enter the message you want to send in your fax transmission. Click Next. The Fax Wizard gives you the opportunity to send an existing file with your fax. Click Next again if you want to skip this option.

4 If you want to include a cover page with your fax transmission, make sure the Yes option is selected on the next window. Then select one of the cover pages from the list below, and click Next.

How to Send a Fax from an Application

Sometimes you may prefer to send a fax document directly from an application. To do so, you simply start the program and prepare the document that you want to send. Then you can begin the transmission process without leaving your current work.

▶ **1** From the Start menu, run the application from which you want to send a fax. For example, start a word processing program, your spreadsheet application, or even the Paint drawing program.

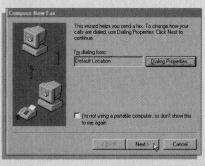

5 The first window of the Fax Wizard appears on the screen. To send your document, go through the steps of the wizard, as illustrated in the previous topic of this chapter, "How to Use the Fax Wizard."

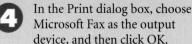

4 In the Print dialog box, choose Microsoft Fax as the output device, and then click OK.

TIP SHEET

▶ **If your application's File menu contains a Send command, you can use it instead of the Print command. Choose Send and then choose Microsoft Fax for sending the message. In response, Windows opens the Microsoft Exchange program. Pull down the Tools menu and choose the Fax Addressing Wizard option to start the steps of the Fax Wizard.**

▶ **There's yet another way to send an existing file as a fax. In the My Computer window or the Explorer, click the file's icon with the right (or secondary) mouse button and choose Send To from the resulting menu. Then choose Fax Recipient and proceed through the steps of the Fax Wizard.**

2 Create or open the document you want to send. For example, type the text of your transmission into the WordPad window, as shown in this figure.

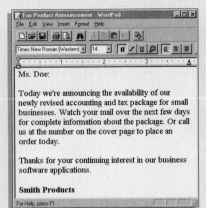

3 Pull down the File menu and choose the Print command. (Alternatively, you can choose the Send command if it is available in this application's File menu. See the Tip Sheet at left for more information.)

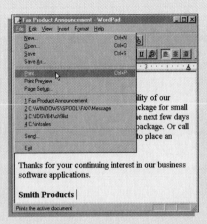

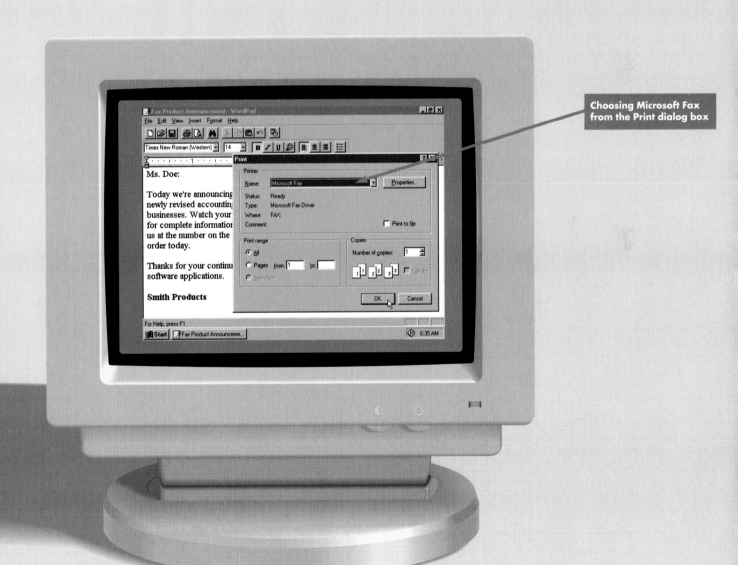

Choosing Microsoft Fax from the Print dialog box

How to Create a New Cover Page

Windows 95 supplies an assortment of cover pages you can use for your fax transmissions. When you send a fax, Windows automatically transfers the appropriate information about your fax location (name, company, phone numbers, and so on) to the standard cover page that you select. But you may prefer to create your own cover page with custom elements that you choose yourself—including your company's logo or any other special information that you want to include. The Cover Page Editor is the tool you need for this task.

1 Click the Start menu and choose Applications. From the list of programs, choose Fax. Then choose Cover Page Editor from the Fax list.

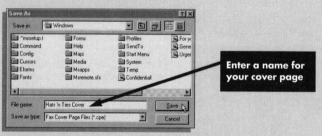

Enter a name for your cover page

6 When you've finished designing your new cover page, pull down the File menu and choose Save As. Enter a name for your cover page, and save the sheet in the Windows directory. (The new file is automatically saved with a .cpe extension.) Next time you use the Fax Wizard, this new cover page will be available as one of the options for transmitting your fax message, as shown on the central graphic on these pages.

TIP SHEET

▶ **To select several fields at once on the cover page, drag the mouse diagonally to form a rectangular frame around the selections. When you release the mouse button, all the fields will be surrounded by selection handles. You can then use toolbar buttons to change the appearance of the selected fields, or you can use your mouse to drag them all to a new location.**

▶ **The Drawing toolbar in the Cover Page Editor provides tools for drawing graphic shapes on a cover page, and for aligning a selection of fields in any direction you choose.**

▶ **For more information about the Cover Page Editor, pull down the Help menu and choose Help Topics. Double-click the Creating Cover Pages book.**

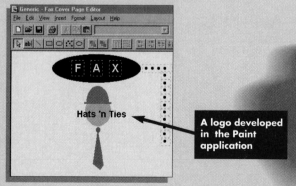

A logo developed in the Paint application

5 If you wish, you can develop a logo or other graphic in the Paint program and paste it to your cover page. (See Chapter 13 for information about Paint.)

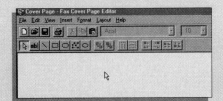

2 The Cover Page Editor begins by displaying a tip sheet. Browse through the tips, if you wish, by clicking the Next Tip button any number of times. Then click OK to close the tip box. On the application window, click the maximize button to give yourself as much room as possible to create your custom cover page.

3 One good way to develop a new cover page is to start with an existing one that Windows supplies. Click the Open button on the Cover Page toolbar. In the resulting Open dialog box, look in the Windows directory. Select one of the cover page files (with .cpe extensions) and click Open.

A custom cover page option

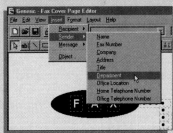

4 A cover page consists of fields that represent the information Windows will transfer to the sheet at transmission time. Rearrange the existing sheet in any way you wish. To select a field on the sheet, click it. To move a selected field to a new location, drag it with the mouse. To delete a field, select it and press the Delete key. To insert a new field, pull down the Insert menu and choose from one of the categories, as shown in this figure.

How to Receive a Fax on Your Computer

As long as your modem is attached to a phone line, you can use the Microsoft Fax software to receive fax messages from anyone who sends them. The source of the message can be an actual fax machine or a computer containing a fax/modem. Once the message has arrived, you can view it on the desktop, send a copy of it to your printer, or save it as a file on disk.

▶ **1** Double-click the Inbox icon on your desktop. (If you don't see this icon, you need to install Microsoft Exchange on your computer. See "How to Use the Fax Wizard" at the beginning of this chapter for more information.) The Microsoft Exchange window opens onto the screen, and a small fax icon appears at the lower-right corner of the Windows 95 Taskbar. This indicates that you are ready to receive faxes or other types of messages. Minimize the Microsoft Exchange window so that it will be out of the way of your other work.

The Save button   **The Print button**

5 A Fax Viewer window opens onto the desktop, showing an image of the fax you've received. Click the Zoom In button on the toolbar to increase the size of the image so you can read your fax. Alternatively, click the Print button to send a copy of your fax to the printer, or click the Save button to save the fax to disk.

> Ms. Doe:
>
> Today we're announcing the availability of our newly revised accounting and tax package for small businesses. Watch your mail over the next few days for complete information about the package. Or call us at the number on the cover page to place an order today.

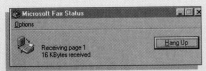

2 When a fax signal arrives, a window named Microsoft Fax Status appears on the desktop. This window reports the progress of your incoming fax transmission. When the fax is complete, the window disappears.

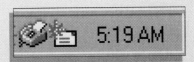

3 As soon as your computer has processed the incoming fax, a mail icon appears on the Taskbar, just to the right of the fax icon. When you want to read your fax, double-click the mail icon.

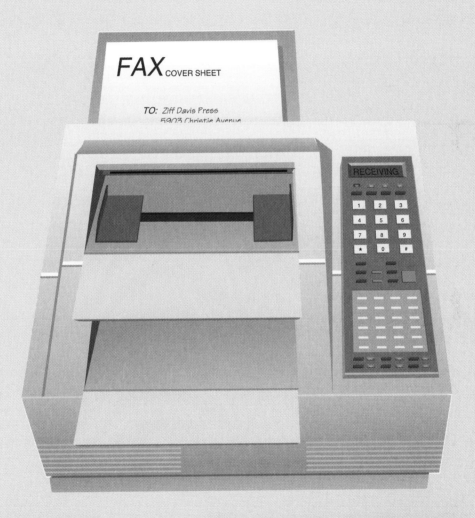

4 The Inbox window appears on the desktop. In the right-hand panel you'll see a description of the fax you've received. Double-click the icon for this message to view your fax.

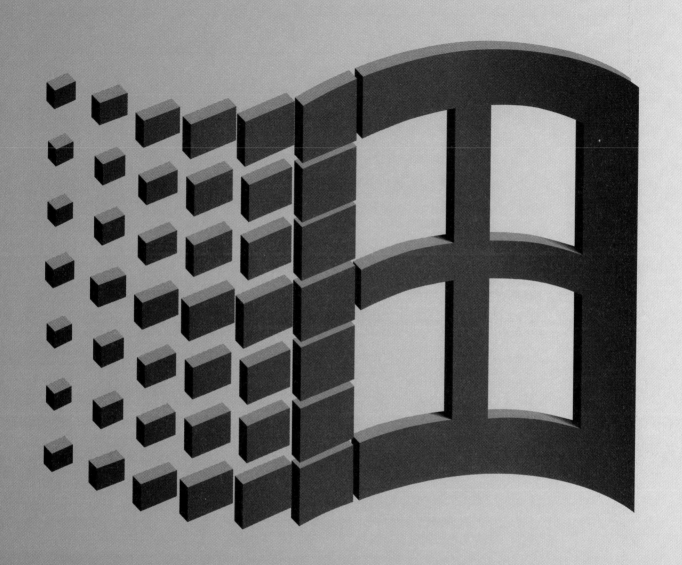

CHAPTER 19

Using the
Microsoft Network

 The Microsoft Network is an online service that offers news, information, special-interest topics, forums, chat rooms, e-mail, Internet access, and more. For a monthly fee, you can become a member and sign on to the Network at any time. When you join, you choose a name to identify yourself in online activities; this name becomes your e-mail address. You also create a password to protect your Network account.

To use the Microsoft Network, you begin by installing the necessary software from your original Windows 95 disk or disks. (See Chapter 16, "How to Add Windows Components," for details.) Then you run a special sign-up program designed to elicit the information needed to set up your new account, including your name, address, phone, and credit card number; and you choose a local phone number for accessing the Network. When these steps are complete you can begin exploring the many services available. This chapter will get you started.

How to Sign Up for the Microsoft Network

The sign-up procedure for Network membership is quick and simple. You supply the necessary account information—including a payment method—and read through the membership rules. Then you create a member name and a password for yourself, and you're ready to begin.

▶ **1** Make sure you've installed the Microsoft Network software from your original Windows 95 disks. Then double-click the Signup icon. If the icon doesn't appear on your desktop, search for it in a folder named The Microsoft Network, located in the Program Files folder. A description of the Network's highlights appears in a window on the desktop. Click OK to continue.

TIP SHEET

▶ **When your membership is approved, you'll be asked to enter a member ID to identify yourself on the Network. You can use your initials, a nickname, or any other name you choose to go by. Your name must be unique—that is, different from existing user names on the Network. (If you happen to enter a name that's already taken by another member, the Network prompts you to try again.) This will be your online name as long as you're a member.**

▶ **You'll also create a password for yourself, to protect your account from unauthorized access. You'll need to memorize this password, and supply it each time you sign on to your account. Once you sign on, you can change your password at any time. Turn the page to find out how.**

The Join Now button

6 Optionally, click the Details button to read more about the Network, and the Price button to learn about pricing for membership. Then if you're ready to proceed, click Join Now. Your account information will be sent to the Network.

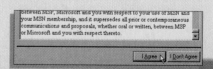

5 Click the third button, labeled "Then, please read the rules." In the resulting window, scroll through the text of the membership agreement, and read the terms. If you're ready to join, click the button labeled "I Agree."

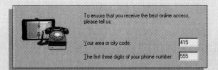

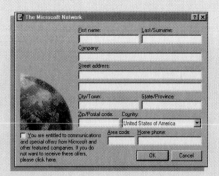

2 In the next window, enter your area code and the first three digits of your phone number so that you can be connected to the Network through a local phone number. Click OK and then click Connect on the next window. The Signup program dials an access number and connects you to the Network.

3 As shown in the central graphic on these pages, a window titled The Microsoft Network appears on the desktop. To join the Network, you need to supply some information about yourself. Click the first button, labeled "Tell us your name and address." Fill in all the blanks in the resulting window, and click OK to return to the main sign-up window.

4 Click the second button, labeled "Next, select a way to pay." In the resulting window, select a type of credit card and fill in the requested information about your own card account. Click OK to continue.

How to Get Started on the Network

A t the beginning of each session, you have the option of changing the local phone number that you use to access the Microsoft Network. This can be a particularly convenient option if you are on the road with a laptop computer and you want to minimize the cost of working online. In addition, different phone numbers are available for the range of standard modem speeds. Once you've logged on, you can change your password at any time; you may want to do so periodically to ensure the security of your account.

1 Double-click the Microsoft Network icon on the desktop. The Sign In window appears, as shown in the central graphic on these pages.

6 Feel free to explore the Network's features now if you wish. (Turn the page for some specific suggestions.) When you're ready to quit, click the Sign Out button on the toolbar.

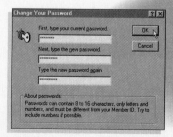

5 If you want to change your password, this is a good time to do so. Pull down the Tools menu and choose Password. In the Change Your Password dialog box, type your current password once and your new password twice to confirm the change. Then click OK.

▶ **Don't forget your password. You can't sign on to the Network without it.**

▶ **Notice that the Sign In window has a check box labeled "Remember my password." Check this option if you want your password to be entered automatically whenever you log on to the Network.**

▶ **When you sign on, the Network notifies you if you've received new mail since your last session. Click Yes if you want to look at the mail you've received. (See "How to Send E-mail" later in this chapter for more information.)**

2 If you want to change the phone number that you use to access the Network, click the Settings button at the lower-right corner of the Sign In window. Click Access Numbers on the resulting Connection Settings window, and then click the Change button for the Primary phone number. The next window lists phone numbers by state or region. Select the number that's best for your location and your modem speed. Click OK on each window to return to the Sign In window.

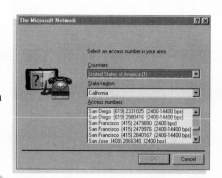

3 When you're ready to connect, enter your member ID and your password into the appropriate boxes on the Sign In window. (As you type your password, the Network window displays a string of asterisks.) Then click the Connect button.

The Settings button

4 The Sign In program dials your local access number and connects you to the Network. The Network Central window, also known as "Home Base," appears on the screen, with access buttons for major categories of services—MSN Today, e-mail, Favorite Places, and so on. If no toolbar appears at the top of the window, pull down the View menu and choose Toolbar. The toolbar contains a varying collection of useful buttons for moving around the Network.

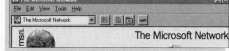

How to Find Network Services

A forum represents a special-interest topic covered on the Network. Each forum includes a variety of features and services. For example, a kiosk provides general information about the forum; a bulletin board is a place where you can read messages and files from other members and post messages of your own; and a chat room is a window in which members carry on live conversations. All the services belonging to a given forum appear in a folder, and each feature is represented by a distinct icon. When you find services that you want to revisit often, you can copy them to your own Favorite Places folder.

TIP SHEET

▶ As long as you remain online, an MSN icon appears at the right side of the Taskbar, just to the left of the time display. If you inadvertently close the Microsoft Network Central window during an online session, click the Taskbar's MSN icon with the right (or secondary) mouse button, and choose Go to MSN Central. Alternatively, double-click the MSN icon on the desktop to reopen the window.

▶ A *Go word* is a shortcut for finding an individual service in the Network. If you know the Go word for a service you want to start, pull down the Edit menu, choose Go to, and then choose Other Location. In the Go To Service dialog box, enter the Go word for the service you want, and click OK. To find out the Go word for a service, select the icon and then click the Properties button on the toolbar. (Alternatively, choose Properties from the File menu.) The Properties window displays the Go word for the feature you've selected.

1 Click MSN Today to find the latest Network news and events. In the Today window you can explore the featured topic by clicking the accompanying photograph or graphic. Return to Home Base by clicking the Microsoft Network application button on the Taskbar.

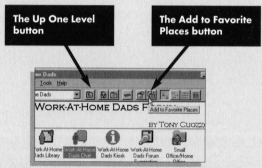

6 Repeatedly click the Up One Level button on the toolbar to navigate back up the folder hierarchy. If you see an icon that you'd like to place in your own Favorite Places folder, select the icon and click the Add to Favorite Places button on the toolbar.

5 Double-click a BBS (*bulletin board service*) icon to view a list of messages and files that members have posted for a particular special-interest topic. Double-click any entry in the bulletin board to read its contents.

The Kiosk icon

2 Click the Categories button at the bottom of the Home Base window. The resulting window shows a collection of folders representing special-interest forums and other services. Double-click a folder to explore a specific forum.

3 When you arrive in a forum folder, begin by double-clicking the Kiosk icon for general information about the forum you've entered. Then click any of the other icons to explore specific topics.

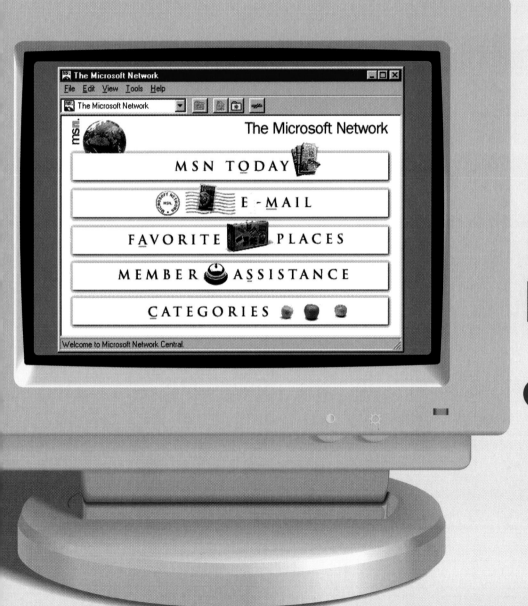

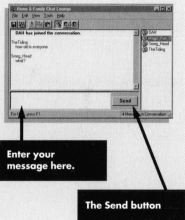

Enter your message here.

The Send button

4 Double-click a Chat icon to participate in a real-time conversation with other members who are also interested in this forum topic. You can enter a message into the pane at the bottom of the window and then click Send to add your message to the conversation. When you're ready to quit, close the Chat window.

How to Send E-mail

The Microsoft Network gives you the ability to send electronic messages—commonly known as e-mail—to other Network members, and to receive e-mail when you log on. Within the Microsoft Network, your e-mail address is simply your member ID. You can also exchange messages with members of other online services, such as CompuServe, Prodigy, and America Online. For this purpose, your e-mail address takes the form *name*@MSN.COM, where *name* is your member ID.

1 In the Microsoft Network Central window, click the e-mail button. When you do so, the Inbox window opens onto the desktop.

6 When you receive a reply to your message—or any other e-mail item—a notice appears when you log on to the Network. To read your message, click Yes and then double-click the message item in the Inbox window.

TIP SHEET

▶ **To send an e-mail message to a member of another online service, enter the user name followed by the *domain name* in the To box. For example, a Prodigy address takes the form *name*@prodigy.com, where *name* is a Prodigy ID such as AABB99A. A CompuServe address consists of two strings of digits separated by a comma—for example, 12345,678. To send a message to a CompuServe member, replace the comma with a period, as in 12345.678@compuserve.com.**

▶ **You can insert an existing file in your e-mail message. In the New Message window, click the Insert File (the toolbar button that displays a paper clip icon), or choose File from the Insert menu. In the Insert File dialog box, locate and highlight the file you want to send. Select a file format from the "Insert as" options. Then click OK.**

5 Click the Send button, the first item on the toolbar, to send your message. (Alternatively, choose Send from the File menu.) If the message is going to another Microsoft Network member, it should arrive almost instantly. Otherwise, arrival time depends on the destination.

The New Message button

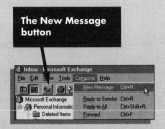

2 Pull down the Compose menu and choose New Message, or press Ctrl+N. (Alternatively, click the New Message button, the third item on the toolbar.) The New Message window appears on the desktop.

3 In the To box, enter the member name of the person you're writing to. Or, if you're sending a message to a member of another online service, enter the person's full e-mail address. (See the Tip Sheet on these pages for more information.) Then enter a brief topic description in the Subject box.

4 Type the text of your message in the large area beneath the Subject box.

The Send button

The Insert File button

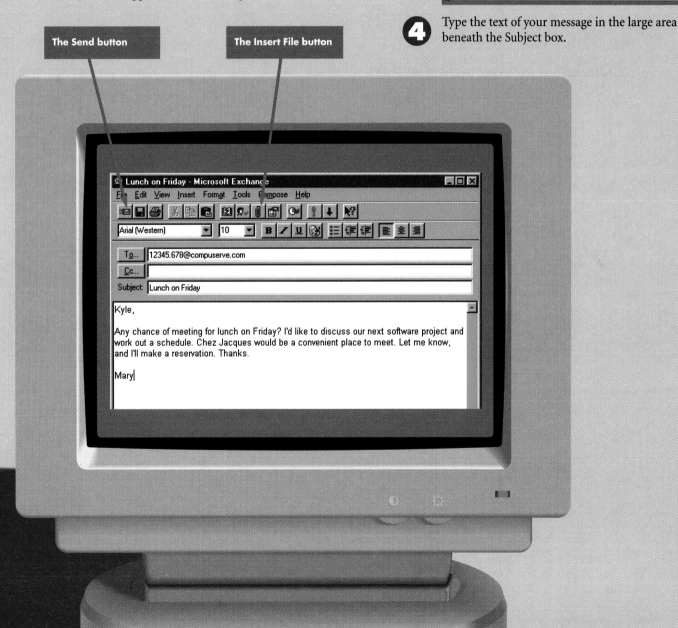

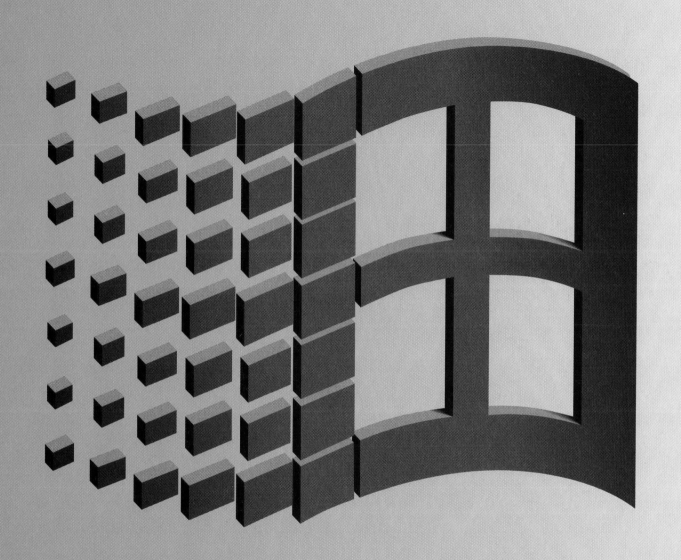

CHAPTER 20

Experiencing Multimedia

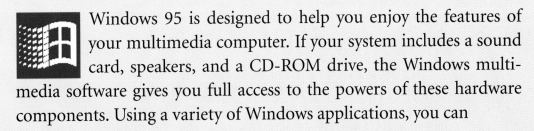 Windows 95 is designed to help you enjoy the features of your multimedia computer. If your system includes a sound card, speakers, and a CD-ROM drive, the Windows multimedia software gives you full access to the powers of these hardware components. Using a variety of Windows applications, you can

- Listen to music on your CD-ROM player while you do other work on your computer.

- Record your own sounds and save them as files on disk.

- View video clips directly on your screen.

To take advantage of these features, begin by installing a selection of the Windows multimedia programs on your hard disk (if you haven't done so already)—including CD Player, Media Player, Sound Recorder, and Volume Control. The Add/Remove Programs utility in the Control Panel guides you through the steps for installing new Windows applications. See "How to Add Windows Components" in Chapter 16 for instructions.

How to Play a Music CD

Using your computer's CD-ROM drive, sound card, and speakers, you can listen to music while you work. Just start the CD Player program and put your favorite music CD into the drive. Like any good CD player, the Windows 95 software allows you to adjust the volume, select a new track, and even create a program of tracks to listen to.

TIP SHEET

▶ If you want the CD Player to play the current CD repeatedly, click the Continuous Play button, the second-to-last button on the CD Player toolbar (see step 2) or pull down the Options menu and choose Continuous Play. When the Player reaches the end of the CD, it will start again at the beginning.

▶ To stop playing temporarily, click the Pause button, located just to the right of the Play button (see step 3). When you subsequently click the Play button again, the CD Player resumes the music where you left off. Alternatively, click the Stop button, located just to the right of the Pause button; when you click Play again, the CD Player starts at the beginning of the CD or at the beginning of your play list.

▶ If you want to restore the original play list (consisting of all the tracks on the current CD), click the Edit Play List button in the CD Player window and then click Reset in the resulting dialog box.

▶ Another way to start the CD Player program is to double-click the CD-ROM disc icon in the My Computer window.

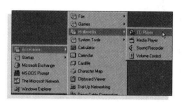

1 To start the CD Player program, click the Start menu, choose Programs, and then choose Accessories. In the Accessories list, click Multimedia and then choose CD Player.

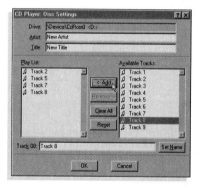

6 If you want to listen to a specific list of tracks—and skip other tracks—click the Edit Play List button (the first button on the CD Player toolbar), or choose Edit Play List from the Disc menu. In the resulting dialog box, click the Clear All button to erase the default Play List. To begin building a custom Play List, select a track from the Available Tracks list and click the Add button; repeat this process for each track you want to include. Then click the OK button. The CD Player plays only those tracks you've included in the list.

5 To switch to a different track on the current CD, pull down the Track list and make a new selection. Windows immediately begins playing at the track you've chosen.

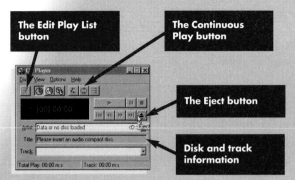

The Edit Play List button

The Continuous Play button

The Eject button

Disk and track information

2 The CD Player window appears on the desktop. If the toolbar, track information, or status bar are missing, pull down the View menu and choose the appropriate options to display these components in the window. Then click the Eject button to open your CD-ROM drive. Insert a music CD and close the drive again.

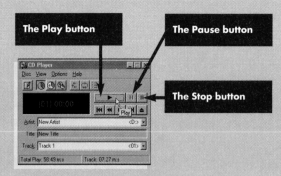

The Play button

The Pause button

The Stop button

3 Click the Play button to begin playing the CD. You can then minimize the CD Player window so it won't get in the way of your other work on the desktop. The music continues playing even when the window is minimized.

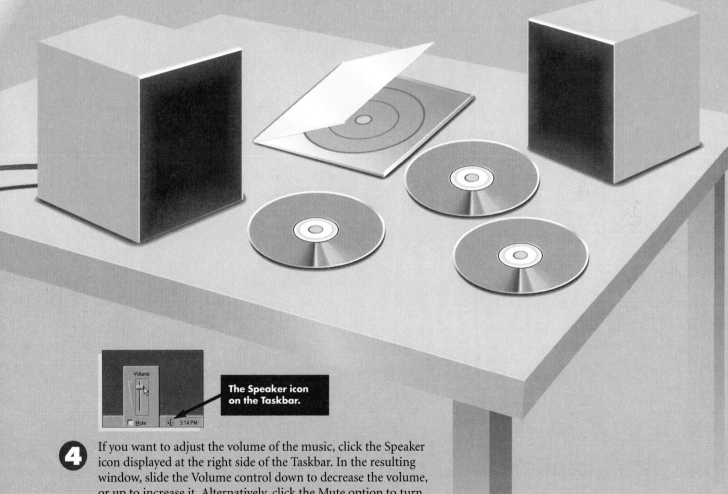

The Speaker icon on the Taskbar.

4 If you want to adjust the volume of the music, click the Speaker icon displayed at the right side of the Taskbar. In the resulting window, slide the Volume control down to decrease the volume, or up to increase it. Alternatively, click the Mute option to turn your speakers off altogether. You can then listen to music privately through a headset attached to your CD-ROM system. On the Taskbar, Windows displays a red circle and slash over the speaker icon to represent the mute mode.

How to Record Sounds

The Sound Recorder program gives you tools to create your own sound files. You can record from a music CD that's currently playing on your CD-ROM drive, or from a microphone attached to your computer. Once you've completed the recording, you can save it as a file on disk and then replay it at any time. You can even paste the sound to another file, where it adds an audio component to the content of a document.

▶ **1** To start the recorder, click the Start button, choose Programs, and then choose Accessories. In the Accessories list, click Multimedia and then choose Sound Recorder. The Sound Recorder window appears on the desktop.

TIP SHEET

▶ When you play back a sound that you've recorded, you can use the options in the Sound Recorder's Effects menu to change the properties of the sound. For example, you can increase or decrease the volume or speed of the sound, and you can even play the sound backwards.

▶ After you create a sound recording, you can copy the sound to the Clipboard by choosing the Copy command from the Sound Recorder's Edit menu. The Copy operation is available whether or not you've saved the sound as a file on disk.

▶ To open a sound file directly from the Sound Recorder, pull down the File menu and choose Open. Find the folder where the sound file is stored, and select the file's name. Then click Open. Back in the Sound Recorder window, click Play to begin playing the sound.

▶ To record a new sound, choose the New command from the File menu. Then click the Record button when you're ready to begin.

Double-click this icon to listen to the sound file in a document.

5 To play any sound file, double-click its icon in the My Computer window. Windows opens the Sound Recorder to play the sound. To incorporate a sound file into another document, click the file's icon with the right mouse button (also in the My Computer window) and choose Copy from the resulting menu. Then open the target document and press Ctrl+V to paste the sound icon. Inside the document, you can double-click the icon to hear the sound.

The Record button

2 Prepare the hardware or device from which you want to record. If you plan to record from a music CD, insert the disc in the CD-ROM drive and start the CD Player. If you're going to record from a microphone, make sure it's attached to your computer and placed in a convenient location for recording. To begin recording, click the red Record button, at the lower-right corner of the Sound Recorder window.

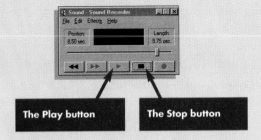

The Play button   The Stop button

3 Click the Stop button (just to the left of the Record button) to stop the recording. Then click the Play button to listen to what you've recorded.

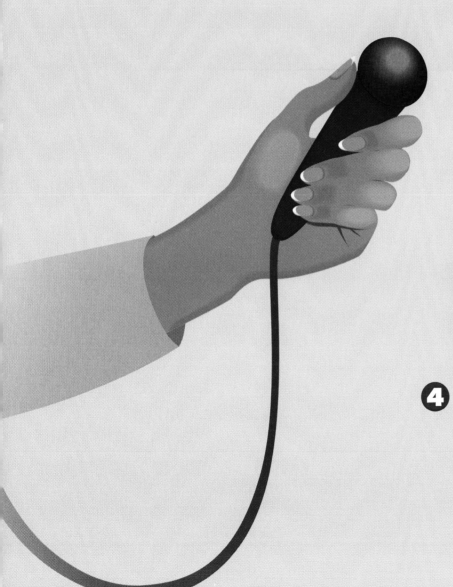

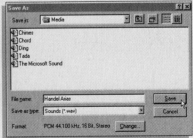

4 To save your recording as a file on disk, pull down the File menu in the Sound Recorder window and choose Save As. Select the folder in which you want to save the recording, and enter a file name. Then click the Save button. The file is saved with a .WAV extension.

How to Play a Video Clip

Video is a dramatic feature of Windows's multimedia capabilities. The Media Player allows you to view a video clip directly on your computer screen and listen to its sound on your speakers. You'll find some sample videos on the Windows installation disk (CD version). In addition, video is a component of many educational and entertainment software packages that you can purchase to run on your computer.

1 Click the Start menu and choose Programs. Then click Accessories and choose Multimedia from the Accessories list. Click Media Player from the Multimedia list.

5 As Windows plays the video, you'll see its images on the screen and hear its sounds from your speaker.

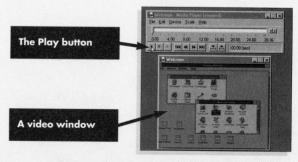

The Play button

A video window

4 A video window opens onto the desktop. Click the Play button at the lower-left corner of the Media Player window to begin the video clip.

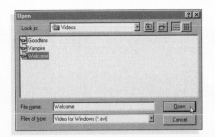

2 The Media Player window appears on the desktop. To view a sample video clip, insert the Windows 95 installation disc into your CD-ROM drive. Then pull down the Media Player's File menu and choose Open.

3 In the Open dialog box, select the CD folder that contains the video clip samples. Then select the video that you want to view and click the Open button.

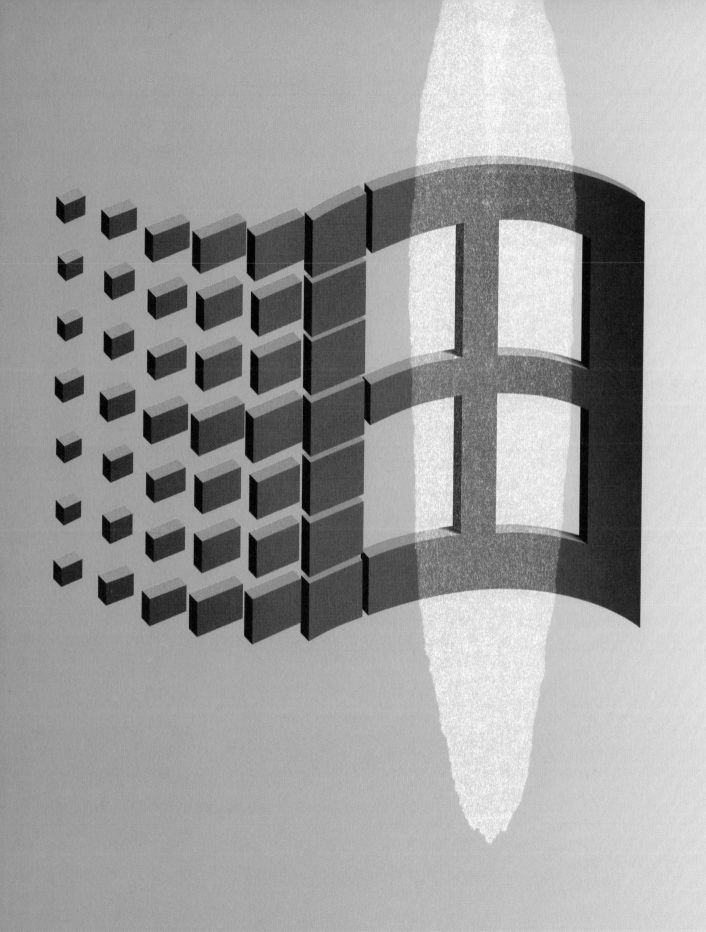

CHAPTER 21

Making Your Computer Accessible

Disabilities in a person's vision, hearing, or mobility can affect the way he or she operates a computer. Always adaptable, Windows 95 provides an important set of Accessibility options to respond to special needs. For example, a choice of high-contrast colors and large fonts makes the desktop easier to read. Audible signals can be reinforced by visual effects on the keyboard. Keyboard adjustments allow a user to type information without having to press multiple keys at once. Other keyboard techniques are available as substitutes for mouse actions.

Although designed to address specific disability issues, these options will appeal to a broad range of users. Like the urban curb cut—meant to facilitate wheel chair access, but also ideal for bicycles, shopping carts, and baby strollers—the opportunity to accommodate personal preferences on the computer is a boon to everyone. Whatever your needs and inclinations, you'll be glad that Windows can adjust to your own style of work.

The Accessibility options are represented by an icon in the Control Panel window. If this icon is not available, you'll have to install this feature from your original Windows 95 disk (or disks). Turn to "How to Add Windows Components" in Chapter 16 for more information.

How to Change the Display

If you have trouble reading text on the screen or seeing activities on the desktop, the Accessibility options offer several solutions. You can choose a high-contrast display (black on white or white on black), or a screen design from the list of preset color schemes. Several of these options provide large text fonts for the elements of the desktop, including the Start menu, title bars, captions, and so on.

- ▶ Most of the Accessibility options have shortcut keys that allow you to turn the options on or off without opening the Accessibility Properties window. For example, the shortcut for the High Contrast Display feature consists of three keys: the left Shift key, the left Alt key, and the Print Screen key, all pressed simultaneously. When you press these keys, a dialog box appears, asking you to confirm that you want to make the change.

- ▶ You can turn off the shortcut for an Accessibility option. Click the Settings button for the target option, and then remove the check mark from the "Use shortcut" option.

- ▶ Another way to change the display colors and fonts is to select options in the Display Properties dialog box. See "How to Select Screen Options" in Chapter 4 for details.

- ▶ If you use the Accessibility options a lot, you might want to place a shortcut to this feature on the desktop. See "How to Create a Shortcut" in Chapter 3 to review the steps.

❶ To open the Accessibility Properties window, click the Start button, choose Settings, and then choose Control Panel. In the Control Panel window, double-click the Accessibility Options icon.

❻ The Notification options allow you to specify whether Windows will display a dialog box—and give an audible signal—when you use a shortcut key to change any of the Accessibility options. (See the Tip Sheet for more information about the shortcut keys for Accessibility options.)

❺ The Automatic reset option gives you the opportunity to restore the original settings after your system has been idle for a specified number of minutes. Check the option and then specify the number of minutes Windows should wait before a reset.

2 The Accessibility Properties window has several tabs, representing categories of system changes. Click the Display tab to select a new appearance for the display screen. Then click the Use High Contrast check box to activate this option.

3 Click the Settings button for more details. The High Contrast color scheme box shows three options for improving the visibility of the display screen—White on black, Black on white, or Custom. If you choose the third of these options, you can also select the specific color and font scheme that will be activated.

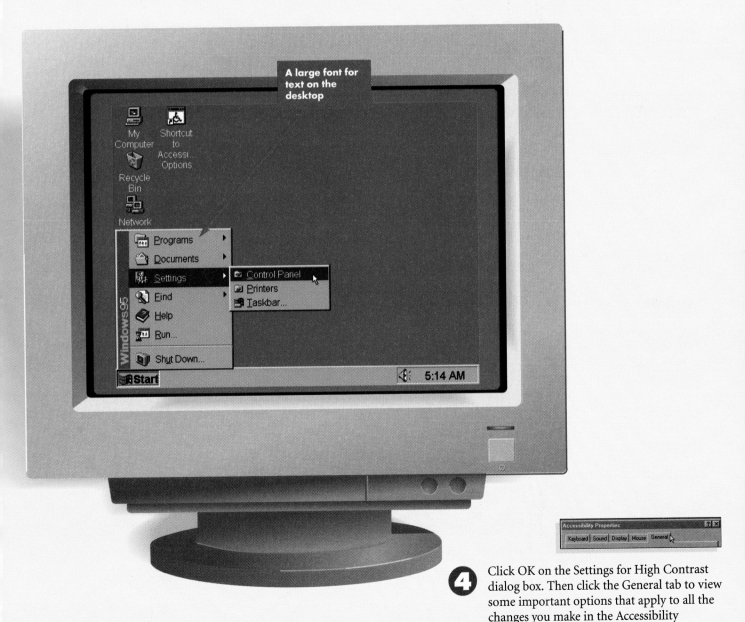

A large font for text on the desktop

4 Click OK on the Settings for High Contrast dialog box. Then click the General tab to view some important options that apply to all the changes you make in the Accessibility Properties window.

How to Change the Keyboard Settings

Windows has many keyboard shortcuts that require the user to press two keys at once, often with one hand. For example, Ctrl+C and Ctrl+V are the universal shortcuts for the copy-and-paste operation; and, of course, capitalization in text requires the use of the Shift key along with a letter key. Some people find these key combinations difficult to carry out. To solve this problem, the *StickyKeys* option changes these shortcuts to sequential keystrokes rather than simultaneous ones; in other words, you press Ctrl or Shift *first*, release it, and then press the second key in the combination. Along with StickyKeys, the Keyboard tab offers two other options, known as FilterKeys and ToggleKeys.

TIP SHEET

▶ **To activate the StickyKeys option directly from the keyboard, press either Shift key five times in quick succession. Then click OK on the resulting dialog box. Windows displays a small icon at the right side of the Taskbar to show when the Ctrl, Shift, or Alt key has been pressed.**

▶ **To deactivate the StickyKeys option, press Ctrl, Shift, or Alt concurrently with any other key.**

▶ **To activate the FilterKeys option directly from the keyboard, hold down the right Shift key for eight seconds.**

▶ **A third option in the Keyboard tab is named ToggleKeys. If you activate this option, Windows produces a sound whenever you press the NumLock, ScrollLock, or CapsLock key.**

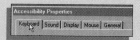

1 In the Accessibility Properties window, click the Keyboard tab. As you can see in the central graphic on these pages, there are several categories of keyboard options.

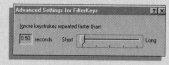

6 Adjust the speed setting and then click OK on each dialog box to confirm this option.

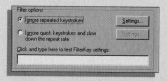

5 Choose between the Ignore repeated keystroke and the Ignore quick keystrokes options, depending upon the kind of keystroke that typically gives you problems. In either case, click the Settings button to specify a range of keystroke speeds that Windows should ignore.

2 Select the StickyKeys option to activate sequential-keystroke shortcuts with the Ctrl, Shift, and Alt keys. Then click the Settings button to examine the StickyKeys options.

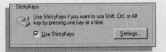

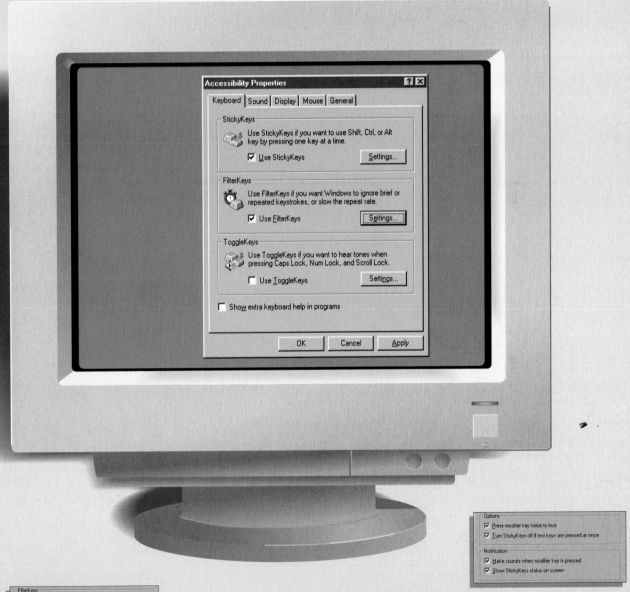

4 If you frequently press keys by accident, the FilterKeys option instructs Windows to ignore certain types of extraneous keystrokes. Select this option and then click Settings to define it further.

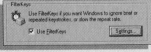

3 The Options box offers techniques for *locking* a modifier key (Ctrl, Shift, or Alt) by pressing it twice, and for turning the StickyKeys feature off by pressing any two keys at once. The Notification box provides sound signals to go along with modifier keys, and a StickyKey icon on the Taskbar. You can activate any combination of these options. Then click OK to return to the Accessibility Properties window.

How to Activate Other Accessibility Options

The Accessibility Properties window offers two other important modifications, known as the MouseKeys and SoundSentry options. MouseKeys allows you to establish keyboard techniques to substitute for mouse actions. You might activate MouseKeys if you find the mouse impractical to use as a pointing device. SoundSentry is designed for users who have trouble hearing the sounds that the computer produces. When SoundSentry is active, Windows provides visual signals along with audible ones.

TIP SHEET

▶ To activate the MouseKeys option from the keyboard, hold down the left Alt key and the left Shift key and then press the NumLock key.

▶ When the MouseKeys option is active, press the Insert key to toggle into the *drag* mode. You can then use the numeric keypad to drag a selected object to a new position on the desktop. Press the Delete key to toggle out of the drag mode.

▶ To read about other MouseKeys actions, choose Help from the Start menu, and search for the MouseKeys topic.

▶ As you can see in the central graphic on these pages, the Settings for MouseKeys dialog box gives you the option of using the MouseKeys option with the NumLock key toggled either on or off. Under the *opposite* NumLock setting, the numeric keypad reverts to its standard use.

1 Open the Accessibility Properties window (by double-clicking the Accessibility icon in the Control Panel) and click the Mouse tab.

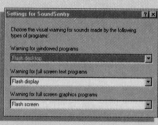

5 In the Settings for SoundSentry dialog box, you can select the display elements that will flash in response to a sound on your system. The first list, labeled "Warning for windowed programs," applies generally to the Windows environment. The other lists apply to specific application environments. Click OK on the Settings for SoundSentry dialog box and the Accessibility Properties window to confirm your selections.

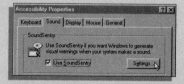

4 Open the Accessibility Properties window again and click the Sound tab. Activate the Use SoundSentry option if you want Windows to provide a visual signal whenever your system produces a sound. Click the Settings button to adjust the details of this option.

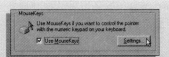

2 Select the Use MouseKeys check box if you want to perform mouse actions from the keyboard. Then click the Settings button to modify the MouseKeys feature. As shown in the central graphic on these pages, you can specify a speed and an acceleration rate for the movement of the mouse pointer.

3 Click OK on both the Settings for MouseKeys and Accessibility Properties windows. Back on the desktop, you can now use keys on the number keypad to move the mouse pointer horizontally (left- and right-arrow keys), vertically (up- and down-arrow keys), or diagonally (Home, End, PgUp, and PgDn keys). When the pointer is positioned over an object on the desktop, press 5 on the number keypad to perform a mouse click, or press + on the keypad to perform a double-click.

How to Set Up User Profiles

If two or more people use your computer, each person can establish his or her own preferences on the desktop. These preferences can include Accessibility changes, along with other options. If user profiles are established, the person at the computer logs on by name each time the system is turned on. Windows keeps track of—and reinstates—the user's preferences.

▶ **1** To begin the process of creating user profiles, click the Start button, choose Settings, and then choose Control Panel. In the Control Panel window, double-click the Passwords icon.

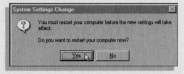

5 A message box entitled "System Settings Change" appears on the desktop. Click Yes to restart your system so that Windows can make the necessary adjustments for your new settings. When Windows restarts, you will be asked for your user name. Type your name, click OK, and then click Yes if you're asked whether Windows should retain individual settings under your name.

2 The Password Properties window appears on the screen. Click the User Profiles tab.

3 Select the option labeled "Users can customize their preferences and desktop settings."

4 As shown in the central graphic on these pages, you can also select a combination of User Profile Settings. (See the Tip Sheet for more information.) Click OK to confirm your new Profile options.

TRY IT!

Now that you've studied the Accessibility options, you might want to explore these features in action on the desktop. In this exercise you'll activate the StickyKeys, SoundSentry, High Contrast, and MouseKeys options, and you'll experiment with their various effects. You'll also review the keyboard shortcuts that Windows provides for quickly turning these options on and off.

Click the Start button and choose Settings. Then choose Control Panel from the Settings list.

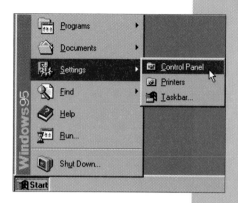

In the Control Panel window, find the Accessibility icon and drag it to the desktop, using the right (or secondary) mouse button. Choose Create Shortcut(s) Here from the resulting menu. A shortcut to the Accessibility options appears on the desktop.

Accessibility Options

3

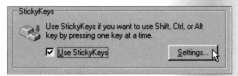

Double-click the shortcut icon to open the Accessibility Properties window. In the Keyboard tab, select the Use StickyKeys option and then click the Settings button. The Settings for StickyKeys dialog box appears on the desktop.

4

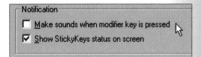

In the Notification box, click the "Make sounds" option to remove the check; with this option turned off, you won't hear constant beeps from your computer as you experiment with StickyKeys.

5

Click the OK buttons in both the Settings dialog box and the Accessibility window to confirm your selections. An icon representing StickyKeys appears on the Taskbar, just to the left of the time display.

6

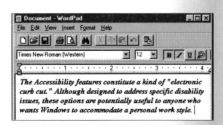

Click the Start button and choose WordPad from the Accessories list. Press Ctrl and then B—as *sequential* keystrokes, not simultaneous ones—to turn on the bold style. Press Ctrl and then I to turn on italics. Then try typing some text. To start a word with a capital letter, press Shift and then the letter.

7

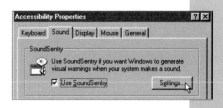

Double-click the Accessibility shortcut again and click the Sound tab. Select the Use SoundSentry option and click Settings.

8

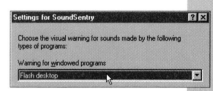

In the Settings for SoundSentry dialog box, choose the "Flash desktop" option in the first of the drop-down lists. Then click OK in both the Settings dialog box and the Accessibility window to confirm your selections.

9

Now turn StickyKeys off by pressing Ctrl, Shift, or Alt along with another key. When you do so, Windows makes its characteristic "turn this feature off" sound and the StickyKeys icon disappears from the right side of the Taskbar. At the same time, the entire desktop flashes momentarily in a new color; this is the effect of the SoundSentry option.

10

Double-click the Accessibility shortcut and click the Display tab. Select the Use High Contrast option and click the Settings button.

Continue to next page ▶

TRY IT!

Continue below

 11

In the Settings dialog box, click the Custom option and choose a color scheme from the corresponding dropdown list. Then click OK in both the Settings dialog box and the Accessibility window.

 12

The desktop displays the new color scheme you've selected, along with any font changes that are part of the scheme. To switch from the new display back to the previous color scheme, hold down the left Shift and left Alt keys and strike the Print Screen key.

 13

Double-click the Accessibility shortcut again and click the Mouse tab. Select the Use MouseKeys option and click Settings.

 14

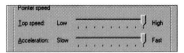

Slide both the Top speed and Acceleration settings to their fastest speeds. Then click OK in both the Settings dialog box and the Accessibility window to activate the MouseKeys option.

 15

A mouse icon appears on the Windows Taskbar, just to the left of the time display. Press the NumLock key once. A circle and a slash appear over the top of the icon, indicating that you've temporarily turned the MouseKeys option off. Press NumLock again to turn it back on.

 16

Experiment with using the numeric keypad to move the mouse pointer around the desktop: Press the arrow keys to move the pointer horizontally or vertically, and the Home, End, PgUp, and PgDn keys to move it diagonally.

 17

Move the pointer to the WordPad button on the Taskbar, and press the 5 key on the numeric keypad to perform the equivalent of a mouse click. This opens and activates the WordPad window on the desktop.

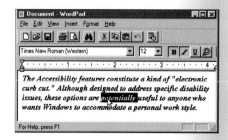

Now move the pointer into the WordPad window, and position it over a single word of text. Press the + key on the numeric keypad to perform a double-click action. In response, WordPad highlights the entire word.

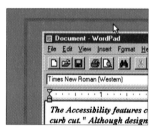

Next try using the MouseKeys feature to drag an object. Move the mouse pointer to the WordPad title bar and press the Insert key on the numeric keypad; this is the equivalent of holding down the primary mouse button. When you next move the mouse pointer position, you'll drag the WordPad window to a new position on the desktop. Press the Delete key to "release" the mouse button and complete the drag action.

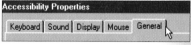

Double-click the Accessibility shortcut icon one last time, and click the General tab in the Accessibility window.

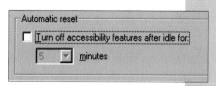

In the Automatic reset box, remove the check from the option labeled "Turn off accessibility features after idle for:" With this option unchecked, your accessibility selections will remain active until you turn them off again.

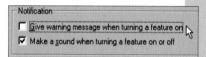

In the Notification box, remove the check from the option labeled "Give warning message when turning a feature on." With this option unchecked, you can use the Accessibility shortcut keys to turn these features on and off quickly and efficiently, without any intervening dialog boxes.

Click OK to confirm your selections in the General tab.

For review, try out the shortcut sequences for the Accessibility options you've worked with: Press Shift five times to turn on StickyKeys; press Ctrl, Shift, or Alt along with another key to turn StickyKeys off. Press the left Alt and left Shift keys along with Print Screen to turn High Contrast on or off. Press the left Alt and left Shift keys along with NumLock to turn MouseKeys on or off.

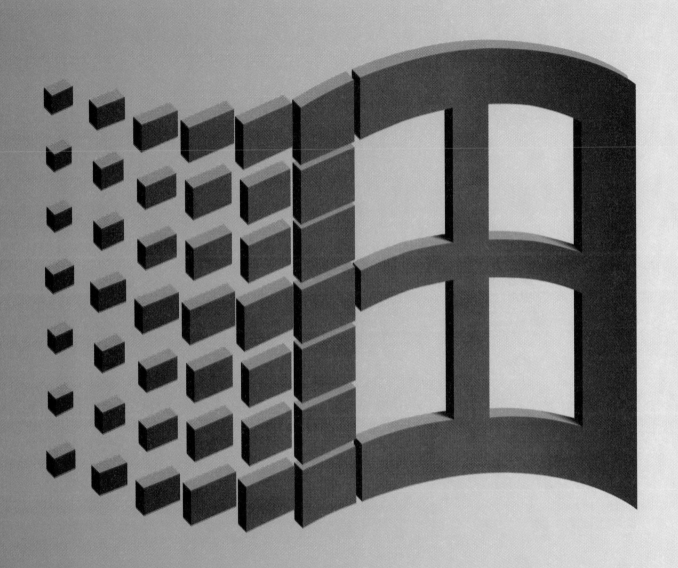

CHAPTER 22

Working with Disks

Windows 95 provides several important "system tools" that will help you maintain and protect the information you store on your hard disk and floppy disks. The Backup program gives you a simple and reliable way to keep backup copies of your most important files. The DriveSpace application increases the capacity of any disk by compressing the information it contains. The Defragmenter and ScanDisk utilities improve the efficiency and integrity of disks and the files they store. You'll learn about all of these tools in this chapter.

A list of these utilities appears when you choose the System Tools folder in the Start menu's Accessories list. If you don't see this folder, you'll need to install these programs from your original Windows 95 disk or disks. Turn to "How to Add Windows Components" in Chapter 16 for installation instructions.

How to Create a Backup

To protect the data you store on your hard disk, you may periodically want to create backup copies of important files or folders, or even of your entire system. The Backup program simplifies this procedure. You begin by selecting the information that you want to save and choosing a destination for the backup set. Once you've created a backup, the program allows you to restore information to your hard disk and to compare the backup copy with the original.

TIP SHEET

▸ **To back up your entire system, first make sure the Backup tab is selected. Then pull down the File menu and choose Open File Set. Select Full System Backup and click the Open button. The program prepares your system for a full backup operation.**

▸ **The Backup program can save your backup set to a tape drive. To see a list of drives that the program can work with, choose Help Topics from the Help menu, and open the category named "Using Tapes for Backup." Then choose "Tape drives that are compatible with Backup."**

▸ **To learn how to restore information to your hard disk from a backup set, turn the page.**

▶ **1** Click the Start button and choose Accessories from the Programs list. Then choose System Tools and click Backup. When you do so, the Welcome to Microsoft Backup window appears on the desktop, as shown in the central graphic on these pages. Read the introduction it contains and then click OK to continue.

6 The Backup utility displays a dialog box showing you the progress of the backup operation. When you see the message "Operation complete," click OK. You can then perform another backup operation, or close the application window.

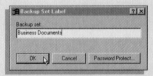

5 In the Backup Set Label dialog box, enter a name for the collection of files you're including in the backup. Click OK to start the backup. The program will create a single backup file under the name that you supply.

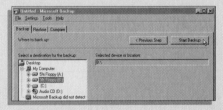

4 Select the drive where you want to store the backup. Then click the Start Backup button.

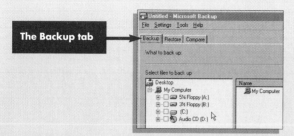

The Backup tab

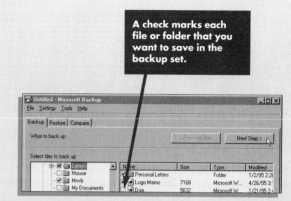

A check marks each file or folder that you want to save in the backup set.

2 The Backup application appears on the desktop, partially hidden by a second window that gives instructions for performing a full system backup. Click OK on the smaller window. Then make sure the Backup tab is selected on the main window. You'll see two adjacent panels for making backup selections; on the left you select disks and folders, and on the right you can select individual files.

3 Click the icon for the disk and/or folder containing files that you want to back up. In the panel on the right, select files that you want to include in the backup, or check an entire folder that you want to back up. Repeat this step for all the folders and files you want to include. Then click the Next Step button to continue.

How to Restore Files from a Backup

If you lose important information from your hard disk, you can solve the problem by restoring original files from a backup set you've created. The Restore tab in the Backup utility allows you to select specific files to copy back to your hard disk from a backup. You can further control the outcome of this operation by selecting options from the Settings dialog box.

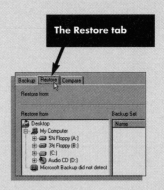

The Restore tab

1 Start the Backup utility by choosing its name from the System Tools folder in the Accessories list. Click OK on the Welcome window and on the small introductory dialog box that appears in front of the application window. Then click the Restore tab in the Backup application window.

5 The Restore window shows the progress of the operation. When the process is complete, click OK.

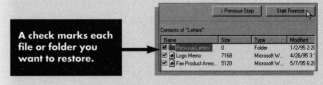

A check marks each file or folder you want to restore.

4 In the Contents list, select the files and/or folders that you want to restore from the backup set you've selected. Then click the Start Restore button.

TIP SHEET

▶ To view the options for the restore operation, pull down the Settings menu and choose Options; then click the Restore tab in the Settings dialog box, as shown in the central graphic on these pages. You can choose to restore files to their original locations or to an alternate folder. You can also specify whether or not the Backup program should overwrite files during a restore operation.

▶ If any errors occur during the restore operation, the Backup program provides information about what went wrong.

▶ You can use the Backup program to compare the files in a backup set with the original files on your hard disk. To do so, click the Compare tab in the application window, select a backup set, and click Next Step. Then select the files you want to compare and click the Start Compare button. The Compare dialog box shows you the result of the comparison.

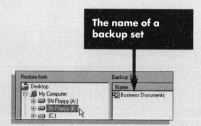

The name of a backup set

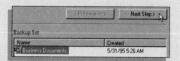

2 In the Restore from list, select the drive where your backup set is stored. In the Backup Set list you'll see the names of the backup set or sets that you've saved on the selected disk.

3 Select the name of the backup set that you want to restore, and then click the Next Step button.

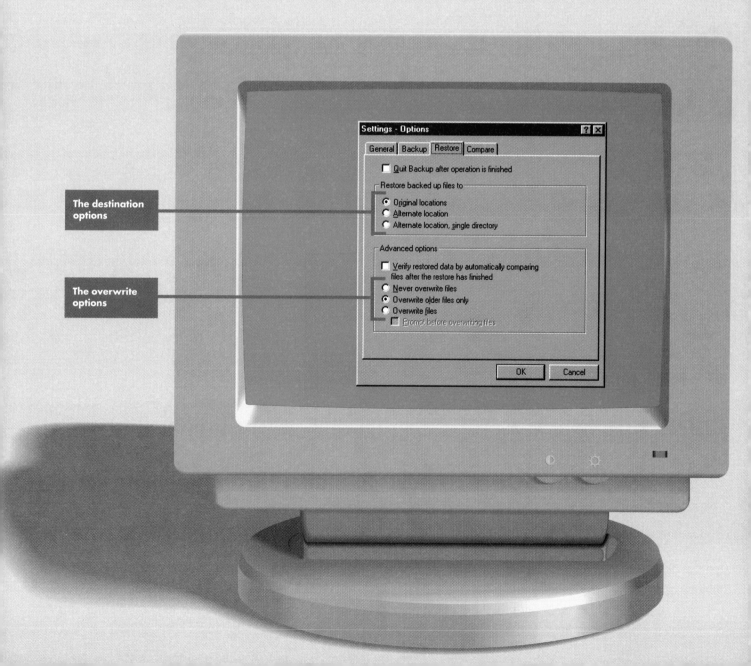

The destination options

The overwrite options

How to Use DriveSpace

A re you running out of room on your hard disk? Do you need a floppy disk with higher-than-standard memory capacity? The DriveSpace utility can help. This program increases storage space through a process known as disk compression. As a result, you can store up to twice as much information on your computer's hard drive or on any floppy disk.

▶ **To view the properties of any drive in the DriveSpace list, select the drive and then choose Properties from the Drive menu (or simply double-click the name of the drive). As shown in the central graphic on these pages, the Compression Properties window tells you whether the drive is compressed and provides information about free space and used space.**

▶ **To increase the capacity of a disk, the DriveSpace program actually creates a file known as a *compressed volume file* on the host drive. To read more about disk compression, pull down the Help menu and choose Help Topics. Open the Overview category and select "Understanding disk compression."**

▶ **DriveSpace is compatible with the DoubleSpace program, a compression utility that was provided with previous versions of MS-DOS.**

▶ **1** Choose the System Tools folder from the Accessories list, and then click DriveSpace. The DriveSpace application window appears on the desktop.

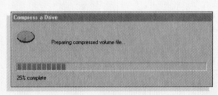

6 The Compress a Drive window charts the progress of the operation. When compression is complete, another window shows the new capacity of your disk.

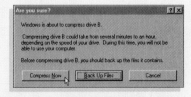

5 A warning message appears next. Read it and then click Compress Now if you're sure you want to proceed.

From the list of available disk drives, select the drive that you want the DriveSpace program to compress.

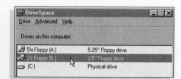

 Pull down the Drive menu and choose Compress. When you do so, the Compress a Drive dialog box appears on the desktop.

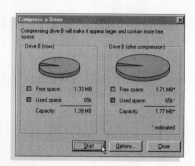

 DriveSpace estimates the amount of additional storage space that will be available on your disk after compression. Click the Start button to start the compression process.

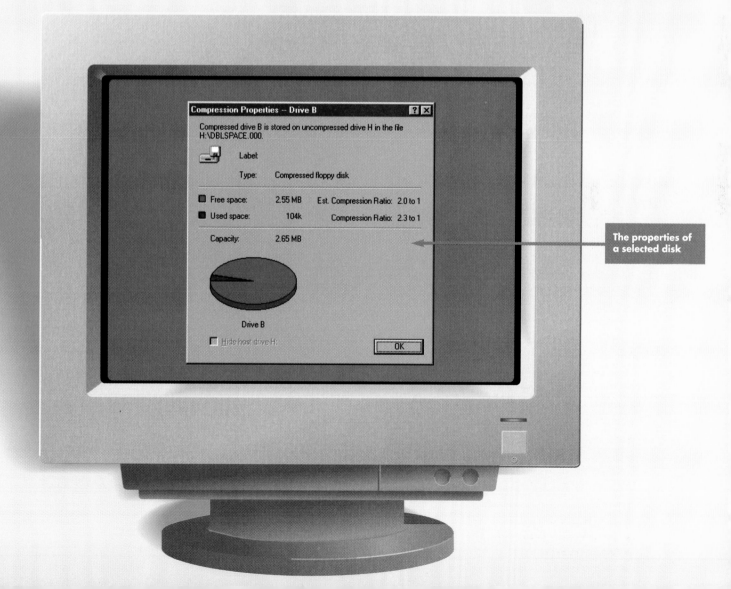

The properties of a selected disk

How to Use ScanDisk and Defragmenter

Two additional programs in the System Tools list are designed to help you maintain the efficiency and integrity of your hard disk or floppy disks over time. The ScanDisk program searches for errors in the files and folders stored on a selected disk, and optionally checks the disk's surface. The Defragmenter rearranges storage, so that each file on a disk is saved in contiguous blocks of space. This results in faster access to the information on your disk.

TIP SHEET

▶ **Fragmentation occurs over time, as you perform many individual save operations on a disk. Due to the changes in available space, files sometimes have to be stored in noncontiguous units. Although fragmented files can always be opened and used successfully, defragmentation generally improves the speed and efficiency of disk access.**

▶ **During the defragmentation process, you can minimize the Defragmenter dialog box and carry on with your other work. When the operation is complete, a dialog box pops up on the desktop; you have the option of defragmenting another disk, or exiting from the program.**

▶ **1** Choose System Tools from the Accessories list, and click the name of the program you want to run.

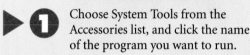

6 Alternatively, click Start to begin. An animated dialog box charts the progress of the operation.

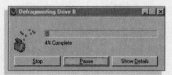

5 A window tells you whether the disk you've selected actually needs to be defragmented at the current time. If the fragmention level is low (or zero), you can skip the operation by clicking the Exit button.

4 To run the Disk Defragmenter, choose the program from the System Tools list. In the dialog box that appears on the desktop, select the drive that you want to defragment, and click OK.

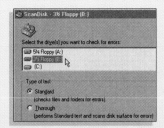

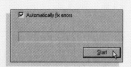

2 To operate the ScanDisk program, begin by selecting the drive that you want the program to check. Then select the type of test you want to perform. The Standard option examines files and folders for errors. The Thorough option includes a test of the disk's physical surface.

3 Select the option labeled "Automatically fix errors" if you want ScanDisk to correct any problems without stopping to prompt you for instructions. Then click Start to begin the test. When the operation is complete, the results appear in a new window, as shown in the central graphic on these pages.

ScanDisk presents an analysis of the disk.

ScanDisk Results - 3½ Floppy (B:)

ScanDisk did not find any errors on this drive.

2,777,088 bytes total disk space
0 bytes in bad sectors
0 bytes in 0 folders
0 bytes in 0 hidden files
106,496 bytes in 7 user files
2,670,592 bytes available on disk
8,192 bytes in each allocation unit
339 total allocation units on disk
326 available allocation units

Close

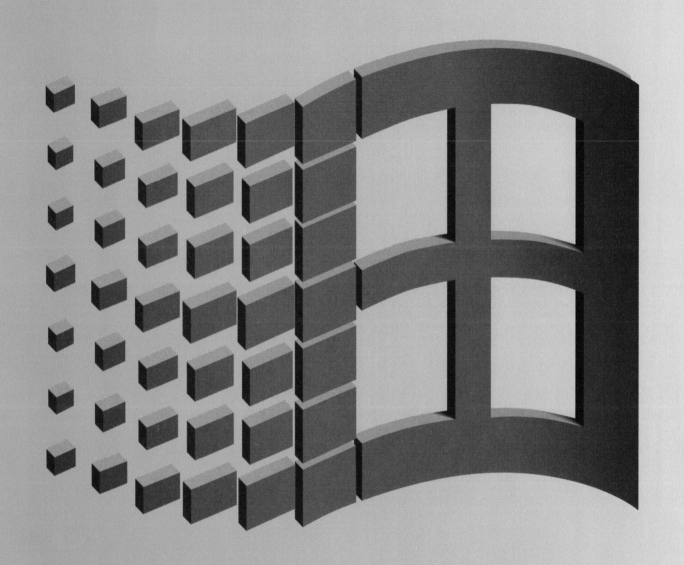

CHAPTER 23

Working in DOS

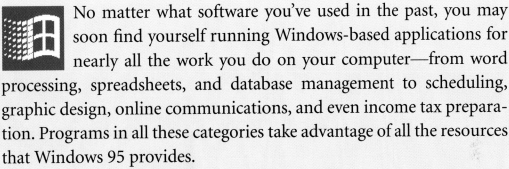 No matter what software you've used in the past, you may soon find yourself running Windows-based applications for nearly all the work you do on your computer—from word processing, spreadsheets, and database management to scheduling, graphic design, online communications, and even income tax preparation. Programs in all these categories take advantage of all the resources that Windows 95 provides.

Still, you may always have a few favorite DOS programs that you'll want to return to from time to time. The MS-DOS Prompt command in the Programs menu conveniently allows you to open a DOS window. In this window, you can run a program or perform a sequence of DOS commands. You can also use the Clipboard to copy information between DOS and Windows applications.

In this chapter you'll explore the MS-DOS Prompt command and begin examining some of its uses.

How to Run a DOS Program

The MS-DOS Prompt command opens an MS-DOS window. In this window you can examine the contents of a disk, copy files, run programs, or perform other DOS-based operations. The MS-DOS Prompt window allows you to work with DOS operations and Windows applications side-by-side on the desktop. You can also switch from the MS-DOS Prompt window to a full-screen view of DOS.

TIP SHEET

▶ **The Mark, Copy, and Paste buttons on the toolbar are for copying text from the DOS window to a Windows 95 application, or from Windows to DOS. Turn the page for more information about these operations.**

▶ **Click the Properties button on the toolbar to open the MS-DOS Prompt Properties dialog box. The tabs on the dialog box represent various categories of special settings you can select for a DOS session. Some of these settings are advanced and technical, but you can do no harm by simply browsing through the dialog box to examine the available options.**

▶ **You can minimize the MS-DOS Prompt window by clicking the Minimize button. When you do so, your DOS window is represented by a button on the Taskbar, just like any other minimized application; click the button to view the window again on the desktop. To close a DOS window, you can type EXIT from the DOS prompt or simply click the Exit button displayed at the upper-right corner of the window.**

1 Click the Start button and choose Programs. From the Programs menu choose the MS-DOS Prompt command. An MS-DOS Prompt window appears on the screen. (If DOS appears in the full-screen mode, press Alt+Enter to switch to the MS-DOS Prompt window.)

6 If you want to switch to a full-screen view of DOS, click the Full screen button on the MS-DOS Prompt toolbar (or press Alt+Enter). Although Windows 95 is still in control, your screen now takes on the appearance of a DOS computer. Press Alt+Enter again to go back to the MS-DOS Prompt window on the Windows desktop.

5 Click the last button on the toolbar, labeled A. In response, Windows opens the MS-DOS Prompt Properties dialog box and selects the Font tab. From here, you can select a new font and point size for the text that appears within the MS-DOS Prompt window. Click OK to confirm your selection and close the dialog box.

2 Inside the window you see the familiar DOS prompt followed by a flashing cursor, indicating that you can now enter commands or run programs. For example, you might use the CD command to change directories and the DIR command to list a selection of files.

3 A special toolbar is available to simplify your work in the MS-DOS Prompt window. If you don't initially see this toolbar, click the MS-DOS icon at the upper-left corner of the window, and choose the Toolbar command from the resulting menu.

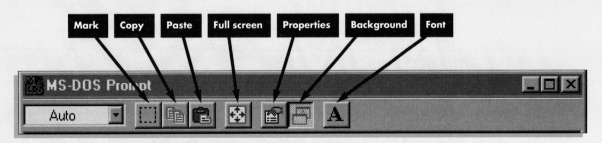

4 The toolbar contains a row of buttons that allow you to perform specific operations within the MS-DOS Prompt window. Position the mouse pointer over each button in turn, and a small ToolTip box tells you what the button does.

How to Copy Information between DOS and Windows

The toolbar at the top of the MS-DOS Prompt window gives you simple ways to copy text from DOS to Windows or from Windows to DOS. Like other copy-and-paste tasks in Windows 95, these operations make use of the Clipboard as an intermediate storage place for the data that's copied.

▶ You can also select copy-and-paste commands from the menu that appears when you click the MS-DOS icon at the left side of the MS-DOS Prompt title bar. First select the Edit command from the menu. The Mark, Copy, and Paste commands in the resulting submenu perform the same tasks as the equivalent buttons on the toolbar.

▶ Windows allows you to open more than one MS-DOS Prompt window at a time. When you do so, you can use the Windows Clipboard to copy information from one running DOS program to another.

1 At the DOS prompt in an MS-DOS Prompt window, use commands or programs to generate the text that you want to copy from DOS to Windows. If the toolbar isn't displayed at the top of the window, click the MS-DOS icon at the upper-left corner of the window and choose the Toolbar command. Then click the Mark button on the toolbar.

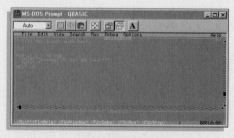

6 Activate the MS-DOS Prompt window and start the DOS program to which you want to copy the text. Then click the Paste button on the MS-DOS Prompt toolbar. This action pastes the text from the Windows Clipboard to the DOS program. In this example, the text has been copied directly to QBasic.

2 Use your mouse to highlight the DOS text that you want to copy.

3 Click the Copy button on the MS-DOS Prompt toolbar. This action copies the selected text to the Windows Clipboard.

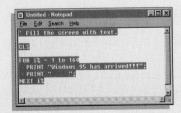

5 To copy information from Windows to a DOS program, begin by activating a Windows application and selecting the text you want to copy. Press Ctrl+C to copy the text to the Clipboard. In this example, the text is part of a QBasic program that's been developed in the Windows NotePad application.

4 Now start the Windows application in which you want to copy the information, and press Ctrl+V to paste the DOS text from the Clipboard.

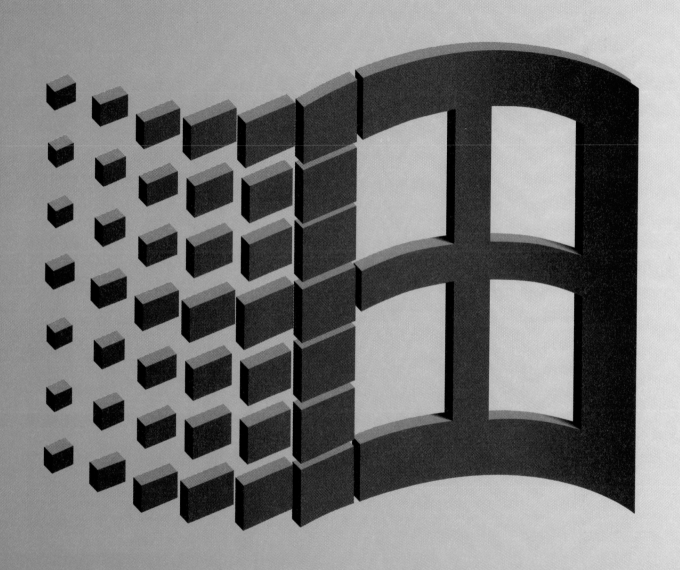

CHAPTER 24

Developing Applications

As you continue exploring the features of Windows 95, you might eventually want to try creating some Windows programs of your own. One way to get started is to install Microsoft Visual Basic on your computer. Whether you're planning to develop a long and ambitious program or just design a few simple software tools for your own day-to-day work, Visual Basic can help you translate your creative ideas into working applications.

Visual Basic doesn't come with Windows; it's a separate package that you purchase and install when you need it. Widely used by professional programmers, this product also proves surprisingly valuable to non-programmers who want to plan the visual components of their own applications.

With a little practice—but no mandatory programming skills—you can learn to create windows, forms, and dialog boxes in Visual Basic. As you complete this initial phase of application development, you'll decide exactly how you want your program to look and behave. Then you have the option of handing your work over to a programmer to complete the project. Alternatively, Visual Basic is a reasonably friendly environment in which to begin learning how to program if you're interested in doing so. Either way, the Visual Basic environment offers a powerful and efficient set of development tools.

This chapter and the corresponding "Try It" section illustrate the major features of Visual Basic. As you read through this material, you'll be able to decide whether or not you want to add this important product to your system.

How to Get Started in Visual Basic

Application development in Visual Basic is a three-step process. First you design one or more *forms* to serve as windows and dialog boxes in your application. These forms may contain *controls* such as command buttons, options, text boxes, menus, and other visual elements that you're already familiar with from your work in Windows. Second, you define the properties of the controls. Properties include visual characteristics such as captions and fonts, along with other options that determine the behavior of controls. The final step is to write the *code*—the Visual Basic commands—to define the specific tasks and actions your program will perform.

TIP SHEET

▶ **Visual Basic applications are *event-driven*. Events take place when the user performs specific actions on the controls in a program. For example, a *Click* event represents the action of clicking a command button with the mouse. When this event occurs, a corresponding event procedure determines the program's response. For example, if the user clicks a button named *Command1*, the event procedure *Command1_Click* is peformed. The code in this procedure defines the actions that will take place in your program each time the button is clicked.**

▶ **To start a new application, pull down the File menu and choose the New Project command. Visual Basic asks you if you want to save the files of the previous project. Click No to abandon any experimental forms you've created during your initial work with Visual Basic.**

▶ **Like any other major software package, Visual Basic has been released in several versions. The screens in this chapter (and in the Try It exercise to follow) are from Visual Basic 3.0, but the steps and instructions will work in other versions of the product.**

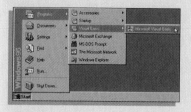

1 When you install Visual Basic on your computer, a Visual Basic folder appears in the Start menu's Programs list. Choose Microsoft Visual Basic from this folder to start the application. As shown in the central graphic on these pages, the Visual Basic environment contains several windows that serve specific purposes in the development process. At the top of the desktop you can see Visual Basic's menu bar and toolbar.

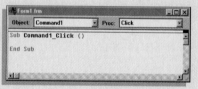

6 When you've arranged a set of controls on a form, the final step is to begin writing code to define your program's operations. To open the code window, you can double-click any control or form. Visual Basic automatically enters the first and last lines of an *event procedure* for the control you've selected. A programmer's job is to complete the procedure by writing a sequence of statements and commands in the Visual Basic programming language. See the "Tip Sheet" on these pages for more information.

The Caption setting defines the text displayed on the face of a command button

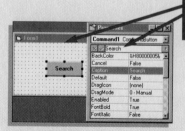

5 The Properties window lists all the properties of a selected control. To change the property settings, click the target control once and then press F4 to view the Properties window. Scroll to and select the property you want to change, and type the new setting. For example, the Caption property of a command button represents the text that appears directly on the button.

2 An empty window named *Form1* is the first form that Visual Basic creates for a new project. By dragging its borders, you can adjust the form's size and shape. Drag the title bar to move the form to a new position on the desktop. You can add more forms to your project by clicking the Form button, the first item on Visual Basic's toolbar. The name of each new form appears in the Project window, which lists all the files in the application you're building.

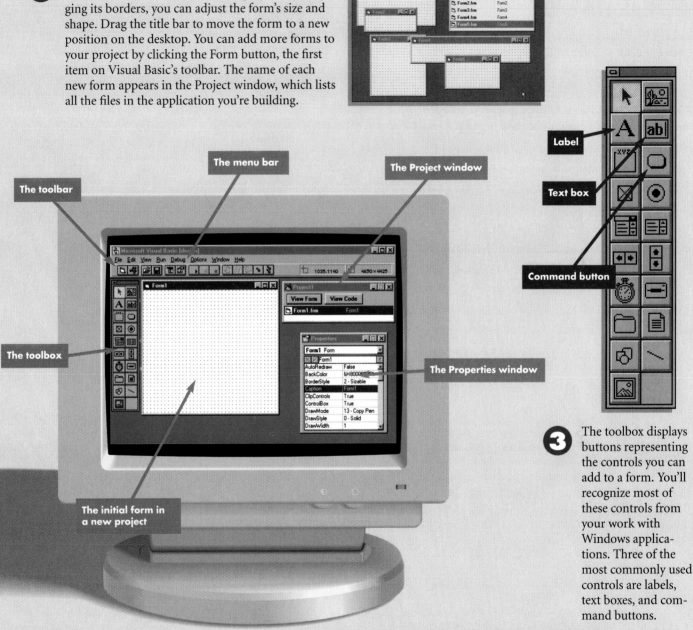

The menu bar

The Project window

The toolbar

Label

Text box

Command button

The toolbox

The Properties window

The initial form in a new project

3 The toolbox displays buttons representing the controls you can add to a form. You'll recognize most of these controls from your work with Windows applications. Three of the most commonly used controls are labels, text boxes, and command buttons.

4 To add a particular control to the current form, double-click the appropriate button in the toolbox. The new control initially appears in the center of the form, surrounded by black *sizing handles*. Drag any of the handles to change the size and shape of the control; drag the control itself to move it to a new position in the form. Visual Basic assigns the control a default name; for example, the first command button you add to a form displays the caption *Command1*. As you'll see in the next step, you can change this caption to identify the button's actual role in your program.

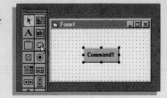

How to Design a Program

When you're ready to begin designing a Visual Basic program, you use the toolbox to select controls for a form and the Properties window to set the properties of each control. Although a complex project may consist of many forms, you can create a useful program with a single form. To save a project to disk, you begin by saving each form file and then you save the project file, which lists the elements of the application. You can *run* a program at any point during the development process. Even before your project contains any code, a trial run will help you see how the program will look on the Windows desktop.

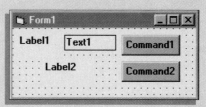

1 Start Visual Basic. As you saw on the previous pages, the default application at startup is named Project1, and it contains a form named Form1. Double-click any buttons on the toolbox to add a selection of controls to the form. For example, the form in this figure contains a text box, two command buttons, and two label controls. Arrange these controls within the form to begin planning the appearance of your application.

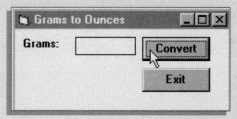

6 Now click the Start button on the Visual Basic toolbar (or press F5) to try running your program. Even though the application contains no code at this point, you can still experiment with the controls you've placed on the form. For example, try clicking the command buttons and notice the visual push-button effect that's built into the definition of this control. Also try entering some information into the text box; notice that you can edit the text by using arrow keys, the Delete and Backspace key, and the Insert key. All these editing operations are built into the definition of a Visual Basic text box.

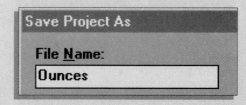

5 Pull down the File menu again and choose Save Project As. This time enter a name for the project file and click Save. At this point, your project consists of two files: the form file and the project file.

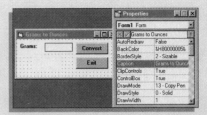

2 Select a control in the form and press F4 to view the Properties window. Change any property settings that affect the appearance of your application. For example, the Text property of a text box defines the initial contents of the box. The Caption property of a command button defines the text displayed across the face of the button. Likewise, the Caption property of a label sets the intial text display. (If you want a text box or label to be blank at the beginning of the program run, simply delete the default entry in the Text or Caption setting.)

3 To change the title bar displayed at the top of the form itself, begin by clicking on an empty spot in the form's background. Then press F4 to activate the Properties window. Scroll to and select the Caption property, and enter the text that you want to appear on the title bar.

4 If necessary, continue rearranging the form and its controls until you've achieved the effect you want. Then pull down the File menu and choose the Save File As command. In the resulting dialog box, enter a name for the form file, and click Save.

How to Learn More about Visual Basic

Visual Basic has a complete and well-organized online help system. As you develop the visual components of an application, you can find detailed help on specific controls and their properties. Then, if you decide to try writing the code for your project, you can get instant help on any keyword in the Visual Basic programming language. As usual, the F1 function key is the tool you use to access help, wherever you are in the Visual Basic development environment.

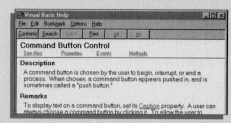

▶ **1** For a complete description of a particular class of controls, select the target control in a form and press F1. The Visual Basic Help window provides detailed information about the control you've selected.

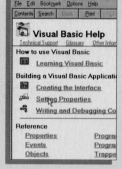

5 To find Visual Basic topics by category, pull down the Help menu and choose Contents. The Help window shows the general categories of information you can read about. Click any underlined topic to open the relevant Help window.

2 To view a list of all the properties that apply to the selected control, click the underlined word *Properties* near the top of the Help topic. In the resulting list, click the name of any property you want to read about; a new Help window provides a complete description of the property. When you've read this information, click the Back button to return to the description of the control itself.

3 To view a list of all the events that apply to the selected control, click the underlined word *Events* near the top of the Help topic. In the resulting list, click the name of any event you want to read about. Then click the Back button to return to the original Help topic, or press the Esc key to close the Help window altogether.

4 If you're working with a project that already contains code—or if you're in the process of writing code for a new project—you can easily open a help window that provides the syntax of any command or statement in the Visual Basic language. Inside the code window, place the cursor next to the keyword that you want to investigate, and then press the F1 function key. The Help window shows you a complete description of the language element you've selected.

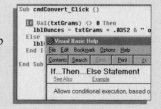

TRY IT!

Here's a chance to try your hand at creating a small but useful Visual Basic program. (Keep in mind that Visual Basic is a separate software package that you need to purchase and install before you can do this exercise.) Imagine that you work for a manufacturing business that has offices both in the U.S. and Europe. From your European offices you regularly receive reports that list product weights in metric grams, and you need a convenient way to convert these measurements to ounces. The solution is a calculation program that you can keep on the Windows desktop where it'll be available any time. You'll be surprised at how quickly you can create this tool.

Click the Start menu and run Visual Basic from the Programs list.

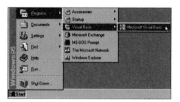

2

In the tool-box, double-click the Label button twice. Two label controls, *Label1* and *Label2*, appear in the center of *Form1*.

3

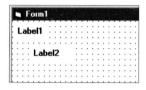

Decrease the size of each label control by dragging the size handles with the mouse. Then move *Label1* to the upper-left corner of the form, and *Label2* to a position just below and to the right of *Label1*.

4

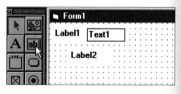

Double-click the Text Box button in the toolbox. The *Text1* control appears in the center of the form. Decrease the size of the box and move it to a position just to the right of *Label1*.

5

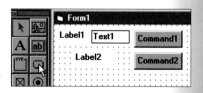

Double-click the Command Button con-trol twice in the toolbox. The controls named *Command1* and *Command2* appear in the center of the form. Decrease their sizes and move the buttons to the right of the other controls you've placed in the form.

6

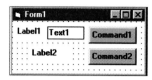

Decrease the size of *Form1* by dragging its borders with the mouse. Then drag the form by its title bar to a position in the approximate center of the desktop.

7

Select the *Label1* con-trol in *Form1*, then press the F4 function key to acti-vate the Properties window.

8

Select the Caption property (if it's not al-ready se-lected) and enter **Grams:** as the new caption for *Label1*.

9

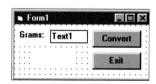

While Caption is still the cur-rent property in the Properties win-dow, select *Label2*, and press the spacebar once to delete the control's current caption. Then select *Command1* and enter **Convert** as its new caption; and select *Command2* and enter **Exit** as its caption.

Continue to next page ▶

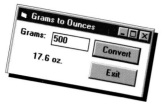

TRY IT!

**Continue
below**

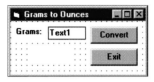

Select *Form1*
by clicking
on a blank
position inside the form, and enter
Grams to Ounces as the form's Caption
property. This new caption appears on
the form's title bar.

⓫

Select the
Text1 con-
trol. In the
Properties
window, se-
lect the Text
property (if
it's not already selected). Delete the
current Text setting and leave it blank.
Then select the Name property and
enter **txtGrams** as the new name for
this text box control.

⓬

While the
Name prop-
erty is still ac-
tive in the
Properties
window, se-
lect *Label2*
and enter **lblOunces** as its new Name
property setting. Then select
Command1 and enter **cmdConvert** as
its new Name setting; and select
Command2 and enter **cmdExit** as its
name.

⓭

Select the
Convert but-
ton and press
F4 to activate
the Properties
window.
Select the
Default property and press *T* to change
the setting to True. (As a result, you'll
be able to use the Enter key to select
this button during a program run.)

⓮

Select the
Exit button
and press F4.
In the
Properties
window, se-
lect the
Cancel property and press *T* to change
its setting to True. (As a result, you'll be
able to use the Escape key to select this
button during a program run.)

⓯

Now double-
click the
Convert button to open the Code window. Visual Basic automatically enters
the *Sub* and *End Sub* lines for the
cmdConvert_Click event procedure.

⓰

Between *Sub*
and *End Sub*,
enter the five
lines of code shown in this figure. Then
close the Code window.

17

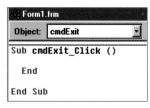

Back on the form, double-click the *Exit* button. In the Code window, enter **End** as a single line of code between *Sub* and *End Sub* in the *cmdExit_Click* event procedure. Then close the Code window again.

18

Pull down the File menu and choose the Save File As command. Enter **Ounces** as the file name for *Form1* and press Enter to confirm. The new file name appears in the Project window.

19

Pull down the File menu and choose Save Project As. Enter **Ounces** as the file name for *Project1* and press Enter to confirm. The new project name appears in the title bar of the Project window.

20

Press F5 to try a first run of your new program. In the Grams text box, type a weight value that you want to convert. Then click the Convert button, or simply press Enter. In response, your program displays the ounce equivalent of the entry.

21

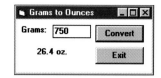

Try other gram measurements; the program provides the correct ounce equivalent for each entry. Press the Escape key when you're ready to quit the program.

22

Pull down the File menu and choose the Make EXE File command. In the resulting dialog box press Enter to accept the suggested .EXE file name. Visual Basic creates an executable program file named OUNCES.EXE.

23

Click the Close button at the upper-right corner of the desktop to exit from Visual Basic.

24

Click the Start button on the Windows 95 Taskbar and choose the Run command. In the Open box, enter the complete path name for your new program, and click OK. The Ounces program starts on the Windows desktop as a stand-alone application.

INDEX

Imagination
INNOVATION·INSIGHT

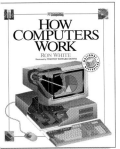

HOW COMPUTERS WORK
RON WHITE

ISBN: 094-7 Price: $22.95
Also available in Spanish.

No other books bring computer technology to life like the HOW IT WORKS series from Ziff-Davis Press. Lavish, full-color illustrations and lucid text from some of the world's top computer commentators make HOW IT WORKS books an exciting way to explore the inner workings of PC technology.

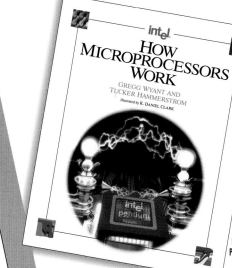

HOW MICROPROCESSORS WORK
GREGG WYANT AND TUCKER HAMMERSTROM
Illustrated by K. DANIEL CLARK

ISBN: 145-5
Price: $24.95

PC Computing

HOW COMPUTERS WORK

INCLUDES INTERACTIVE CD-ROM

RON WHITE
Illustrated by TIMOTHY EDWARD DOWNS

ISBN: 250-8   Price: $39.95

HOW COMPUTER PROGRAMMING WORKS
DANIEL APPLEMAN
Illustrated by SARAH ISHIDA

ISBN: 195-1   Price: $24.95

HOW DESKTOP PUBLISHING WORKS
PAMELA PFIFFNER AND BRUCE FRASER
Illustrated by DAVE FEASEY

ISBN: 191-9
Price: $24.95

HOW WINDOWS WORKS
KAARE CHRISTIAN
Illustrated by PAMELA DRURY WATTENMAKER

ISBN: 193-5   Price: $24.95

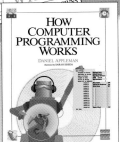

HOW MULTIMEDIA WORKS
ERIK HOLSINGER
Illustrated by STEPHEN ADAMS

ISBN: 208-7   Price: $24.95

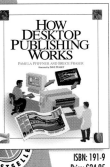

HOW THE INTERNET WORKS
JOSHUA EDDINGS
Illustrated by PAMELA DRURY WATTENMAKER

ISBN: 192-7   Price: $24.95

ZIFF-DAVIS
ZD PRESS

Available at all fine bookstores or by calling 1-800-688-0448, ext. 100. Call for more information on the Instructor's Supplement, including transparencies for each book in the *How It Works* Series. For Corporate/Government programs, call (800) 488-8741 ext. 297. For Education programs, call (800) 786-6541.

© 1994 Ziff-Davis Press

See.

It's that simple.

Just open these colorfully illustrated guide-books and watch the answers to your software questions unfold.

The HOW TO USE books from Ziff-Davis Press make computing easy by presenting each task visually on two facing pages. You'll see what you want to achieve, and exactly how to achieve it.

There's no guess work. The HOW TO USE books are the affordable alternative for those of us who would rather let the computer do the work.

For more information call (800) 688-0448, ext. 253. For Corporate/ Government programs, call (800) 488-8741 ext. 297. For Education programs, call (800) 786-6541.

HOW TO USE MICROSOFT WORKS

ISBN: 1-56276-214-1
Price: $17.95

HOW TO USE EXCEL

ISBN: 1-56276-185-4
Price: $17.95

HOW TO USE THE INTERNET

ISBN: 1-56276-222-2
Price: $17.95

ZIFF-DAVIS ZD PRESS

© 1994
Ziff-Davis Press

Cut Here

Cut Here

Ziff-Davis Press Survey of Readers

Please help us in our effort to produce the best books on personal computing.
For your assistance, we would be pleased to send you a FREE catalog
featuring the complete line of Ziff-Davis Press books.

1. How did you first learn about this book?

Recommended by a friend . . . . ☐ -1 (5)

Recommended by store personnel . . . . ☐ -2

Saw in Ziff-Davis Press catalog . . . . ☐ -3

Received advertisement in the mail . . . . ☐ -4

Saw the book on bookshelf at store . . . . ☐ -5

Read book review in: _____ ☐ -6

Saw an advertisement in: _____ ☐ -7

Other (Please specify): _____ ☐ -8

2. Which THREE of the following factors most influenced your decision to purchase this book? (Please check up to THREE.)

Front or back cover information on book . . . ☐ -1 (6)

Logo of magazine affiliated with book . . . . . . ☐ -2

Special approach to the content . . . . ☐ -3

Completeness of content . . . . ☐ -4

Author's reputation. ☐ -5

Publisher's reputation . . . . ☐ -6

Book cover design or layout . . . . ☐ -7

Index or table of contents of book . . . . ☐ -8

Price of book . . . . ☐ -9

Special effects, graphics, illustrations . . . . . . ☐ -0

Other (Please specify): _____ ☐ -x

3. How many computer books have you purchased in the last six months? _____ (7-10)

4. On a scale of 1 to 5, where 5 is excellent, 4 is above average, 3 is average, 2 is below average, and 1 is poor, please rate each of the following aspects of this book below. (Please circle your answer.)

Depth/completeness of coverage	5	4	3	2	1	(11)
Organization of material	5	4	3	2	1	(12)
Ease of finding topic	5	4	3	2	1	(13)
Special features/time saving tips	5	4	3	2	1	(14)
Appropriate level of writing	5	4	3	2	1	(15)
Usefulness of table of contents	5	4	3	2	1	(16)
Usefulness of index	5	4	3	2	1	(17)
Usefulness of accompanying disk	5	4	3	2	1	(18)
Usefulness of illustrations/graphics	5	4	3	2	1	(19)
Cover design and attractiveness	5	4	3	2	1	(20)
Overall design and layout of book	5	4	3	2	1	(21)
Overall satisfaction with book	5	4	3	2	1	(22)

5. Which of the following computer publications do you read regularly; that is, 3 out of 4 issues?

Byte . . . . ☐ -1 (23)

Computer Shopper . . . . ☐ -2

Corporate Computing . . . . ☐ -3

Dr. Dobb's Journal . . . . ☐ -4

LAN Magazine . . . . ☐ -5

MacWEEK . . . . ☐ -6

MacUser . . . . ☐ -7

PC Computing . . . . ☐ -8

PC Magazine . . . . ☐ -9

PC WEEK . . . . ☐ -0

Windows Sources . . . . ☐ -x

Other (Please specify): _____ ☐ -y

Please turn page.

PLEASE TAPE HERE ONLY—DO NOT STAPLE

6. What is your level of experience with personal computers? With the subject of this book?

	With PCs	With subject of book
Beginner.	☐ -1 (24)	☐ -1 (25)
Intermediate.	☐ -2	☐ -2
Advanced.	☐ -3	☐ -3

7. Which of the following best describes your job title?

Officer (CEO/President/VP/owner). . . . . . . ☐ -1 (26)
Director/head. . . . . ☐ -2
Manager/supervisor. . . . . ☐ -3
Administration/staff. . . . . ☐ -4
Teacher/educator/trainer. . . . . ☐ -5
Lawyer/doctor/medical professional. . . . . . ☐ -6
Engineer/technician. . . . . ☐ -7
Consultant. . . . . ☐ -8
Not employed/student/retired. . . . . ☐ -9
Other (Please specify): _____ ☐ -0

8. What is your age?

Under 20. . . . . ☐ -1 (27)
21-29. . . . . ☐ -2
30-39. . . . . ☐ -3
40-49. . . . . ☐ -4
50-59. . . . . ☐ -5
60 or over. . . . . ☐ -6

9. Are you:

Male. . . . . ☐ -1 (28)
Female. . . . . ☐ -2

Thank you for your assistance with this important information! Please write your address below to receive our free catalog.

Name: _____

Address: _____

City/State/Zip: _____

Fold here to mail.

2680-08-14

NO POSTAGE NECESSARY IF MAILED IN THE UNITED STATES

BUSINESS REPLY MAIL
FIRST CLASS MAIL   PERMIT NO. 1612   OAKLAND, CA

POSTAGE WILL BE PAID BY ADDRESSEE

Ziff-Davis Press
5903 Christie Avenue
Emeryville, CA 94608-1925
Attn: Marketing